Andrew Brown is a freelance journalist who writes extensively for the *Independent*, the *Sunday Telegraph* and the *Daily Mail*. In 1995 he won the Templeton Prize as the best religious affairs correspondent in Europe. He is the author of a highly acclaimed book on the London Metropolitan police called *Watching the Detectives*.

The Darwin Wars

The Scientific Battle for the Soul of Man

Andrew Brown

TOUCHSTONE

SIMON &
SCHUSTER

First published in Great Britain by Simon & Schuster UK Ltd, 1999
This edition first published by Touchstone, 2000
An imprint of Simon & Schuster UK Ltd
A Viacom company

Copyright © Andrew Brown, 1999

This book is copyright under the Berne Convention.
No reproduction without permission.
® and © 1997 Simon & Schuster Inc. All rights reserved.
Touchstone & Design is a registered trademark of Simon & Schuster Inc

The right of Andrew Brown to be identified as author of this work has been
asserted by him in accordance with sections 77 and 78 of the Copyright,
Designs and Patents Act, 1988.

3 5 7 9 10 8 6 4 2

Simon & Schuster UK Ltd
Africa House
64–78 Kingsway
London WC2B 6AH

Simon & Schuster Australia
Sydney

A CIP catalogue record for this book is available from the British Library.

ISBN 0-684-85145-8

Typeset by SX Composing DTP, Rayleigh, Essex
Printed and bound in Great Britain by Cox & Wyman, Ltd.

The current disputes in evolutionary biology differ in no important respects from other scientific controversies. Accusations of rediscovering the wheel, beating dead horses, attacking straw men, and parodying the views of one's opponents have been ubiquitous . . . . No disinterested, non-committal, theory-free characterisation of such events is possible.
David Hull, *Science as a Process*

Violent zeal for truth hath an hundred to one odds to be either petulancy, ambition, or pride.
Jonathan Swift, *Apophthegms and Maxims*

Evolution is to analogy as statues are to birdshit.
Steve Jones, *New York Review of Books*

CONTENTS

FOREWORD

GOD, WHEN HE died, left many situations vacant. Science has nowadays the prestige that theology once had as a source of authoritative answers to such questions as 'Who are we?', 'Why are we here?' and others whose answers are not strictly factual or even numerical. It has also inherited much of the capacity for hatred traditionally engendered by long study of God, truth, or beauty. This is not an entirely new development. In the twentieth century the prestige of science has been borrowed to justify everything from totalitarianism (or 'scientific socialism') to dodgy and litigious religions. But in the last thirty years, the resurgence of Darwinian explanations has provided a particularly potent brew of good science, striking metaphors, and bad philosophy, and consequently savage and important discussions.

Scientific disputes have always been acrimonious. Scientists are not generally kinder or less arrogant than the general run of humanity. But the Darwin wars – the disputes over the scope and importance of evolutionary explanations in the world – have been nastier than most. This is fundamentally because they are disagreements about the nature and importance of mankind. Explanations based on genes and evolution have spread to cover almost every area of science and popular culture in the last thirty years.

Since their subject matter is so important, getting it right is rewarded with great fame and large amounts of money. The splendour of these prizes does something to explain the ferocity with which they are fought over. But there is more. These struggles have political implications which affect all sorts of ways in which human society could or should be organised. Must private property be a fundamental feature of any workable society? Or sexual equality? Must a happy society be religious?

You can give Darwinian answers to all those questions: but the answers will not necessarily be the same; nor even consistent with each other. Darwinian beliefs have been used to justify anarchy, fascism, liberal capitalism, and almost anything in between. But all these justifications are agreed on one thing: that there is a human nature, and the study of our evolution can help us discover how we ought to live. In that sense, Darwinism is irrevocable. Once we have started to understand ourselves as animals adapted for particular ways of life, it is impossible to go back to earlier ideas.

But the large-scale implications of modern biology are only part of these controversies. It is important that the power of genetics has become contested on broadly political lines, so that enthusiasts for the project will be right-liberal, and their opponents, Marxists or influenced by Marxism. But that in itself would not explain why the disputes have been so heartfelt and vicious. The other important quality that they have is that they apply on small scales as well as large. Beliefs about evolution are not just beliefs about society and about humanity in general. They are also specific beliefs about the believers. This is another way in which they resemble theological questions. Just as the theologian is always discussing his own chances of damnation or salvation, which give an unmistakable urgency to his controversial opinions, so anyone who looks at the Darwinian explanations for human life is also talking about them.

I don't believe that science and religion need be two deadly enemies, or even that they deal with the same subject matter. But the ideas of the Darwinian revolution straddle the boundaries between the two and the contending theories in this book are certainly struggling for the soul of every reader.

ACKNOWLEDGEMENTS

My thanks to all the people who talked to me about their parts in these events, especially Richard Dawkins, Bill Hamilton, Mary Midgley and John Maynard Smith. Also to Jeremy Ahouse, Oliver Morton, Tom Wilkie and Jackie Leach Scully, who did their various best to stop me making a fool of myself. With help like that, any mistakes which remain must be ascribed to stupidity rather than ignorance. Without the enthusiasm and energy of Georgina Capel there would be no book at all. My editors, Ingrid Connell and Helen Simpson, have done nice cop and nasty cop to perfection: Ingrid's the nice one, Helen is the best copy editor I can imagine. My wife, Caroline, has also copy edited this. That is not all she has done.

Thanks are due to the following for permission to reproduce copyright material: the Society of Authors as the Literary Representative of the Estate of A.E. Housman for permission to reprint extracts from 'Here Dead We Lie' and Poem No. 9 in *Last Poems*. Cambridge University Press, excerpts from 'Gene Juggling' by Mary Midgely in *Philosophy*, No. 54, 1979, and from 'In Defence of Selfish Genes' by Richard Dawkins in *Philosophy*, No. 56, 1981. Leda Cosmides and John Tooby, excerpts from an unpublished letter sent to the *New York Review of Books*, 1998. W.H. Freeman and Company, excerpt from *The Extended Phenotype* by Richard Dawkins © 1982 by W. H. Freeman and Company. Used with permission of W. H. Freeman and Company, New York, excerpt from *The Collected Papers of W. D. Hamilton: Narrow Roads of Gene Land, Vol. 1, Evolution of Social Behaviour* © 1996 by W. D. Hamilton. HarperCollins, excerpt from *Darwin and the Spirit of Man* by Alister Hardy, 1984. Oxford University Press, excerpts from *The Selfish Gene* by Richard Dawkins, 1989 edition. Penguin Books, excerpt from *The Doctrine of DNA: Biology as Ideology* by R. C. Lewontin (Penguin Books, 1993) © R. C. Lewontin and the Canadian Broadcasting Corporation, 1991. Reproduced by permission of Penguin Books Ltd, excerpts from *The Naturalist* by Edward O. Wilson (Penguin Books, 1996) © 1994 by Island Press.

1

THE DEATHBED OF AN ALTRUIST

GEORGE PRICE KILLED himself in a squat near Euston station in the winter of 1974. William Hamilton, who identified Price's body, has described the scene:

'A mattress on the floor, one chair, a table, and several ammunition boxes made the only furniture. Of all the books and furnishings that I remembered from our first meeting in his fairly luxurious flat near Oxford Circus there remained some cheap clothes, a two-volume copy of Proust, and his typewriter. A cheap suitcase, and some cardboard boxes contained most of his papers, others were scattered about on ammunition chests.'[1]

The deathbed of an altruist can be a terrible place. Both Price and Hamilton were theoretical biologists, a discipline about as mathematical and abstruse as may be imagined; yet it was Price's discoveries in the field which had led to his despair and death. He had reformulated a set of mathematical equations that shows how altruism can prosper in a world where it seems that only selfishness is rewarded. The equations had been discovered ten years before by Hamilton, but Price's reworking was more elegant and of

---

1 Hamilton, *Narrow Roads of Gene Land*, p. 174.

wider application. He had provided a general way in which to measure the direction and speed of any selection process; this makes possible, in principle, a Darwinian analysis of almost anything.

When Price had first found them he was so shocked that he set himself to do the work again, sure that there must be a flaw. He ended up reformulating them more generally and more powerfully; when this work was completed, he went mad. For though his equation showed that truly self-sacrificing behaviour can exist among animals, and even humans, it also seemed to show that there is nothing noble in it. Only behaviour which helps to spread the genes that cause it can survive in the very long term. Since man, too, is an animal, the human capacity for altruism must be strictly limited; and our capacity for cruelty, treachery and selfishness impossible to eradicate. Through algebra, George Price had found proof of original sin.

Before then, he had been a dogmatic and optimistic atheist; he seems to have hoped that man might become better and wiser, perhaps slowly, fitfully and with reverses; but with no natural limit to the process. His proof that this could not happen contains, to a mathematically literate biologist, great beauty and elegance, but it also seems to contain the proof that beauty and elegance mean nothing to the universe. Since human motivation is a complex and difficult matter, one cannot say exactly what drove Price mad. But there is no doubt that the discovery of the equation for altruism plunged him into a profound and severe depression, from which he was rescued by a religious experience which led him into a mania for good.

In an overwhelming moment of spontaneous prayer, just north of BBC Broadcasting House, Price became convinced that Christianity was true. The absolute and unconditional altruism that Jesus preached in the parable of the Good Samaritan was to guide the rest of his life. He did not abandon his scientific work; indeed, he came to consider his discovery a miracle, for he had no training in biology. But he also began to help tramps, alcoholics, and all the wretched of the earth. He gave them time, sympathy, and money – eventually everything he owned.

As an atheist and materialist, Price had been an insufferable zealot; as a Christian, he was just the same. He soon quarrelled with the priest who received him, whom he found insufficiently zealous. He was not a fundamentalist in any normal sense: he completely accepted Darwinian evolution, and continued to work on his equation. He did not believe in the literal truth of the creation narratives. But he followed the voice of Jesus as directly and doggedly as an ant follows the trail its colony has laid down for it.

'This has been a rather trying period for me', he wrote to one of his collaborators, the distinguished theoretical biologist John Maynard Smith, in the autumn of 1972, about a year after his breakdown. 'You can probably guess in what way I mean. I think I told you when you were here that I preached a sermon last year in which I gave a somewhat new explanation of Matthew 6: 25–34.' This is the passage in which Jesus says:

> *Do not worry about your life, what you will eat or drink; or about your body, what you will wear. Is not life more important than food, and the body more important than clothes?*
>
> *Look at the birds of the air; they do not sow or reap or store away in barns, and yet your heavenly Father feeds them. Are you not much more valuable than they?*
>
> *Who of you by worrying can add a single hour to his life?*
>
> *'And why do you worry about clothes? See how the lilies of the*

field grow. They do not labour or spin.
Yet I tell you that not even Solomon in all his splendour was
dressed like one of these.
If that is how God clothes the grass of the field, which is here
today and tomorrow is thrown into the fire, will he not much
more clothe you, O you of little faith?
So do not worry, saying, 'What shall we eat?' or 'What shall
we drink?' or 'What shall we wear?'

'At one point in the sermon I said something to the effect
that "I hold an ordinary job, live in an ordinary flat, dress
conventionally, am paid a regular salary." I *sort of* knew back
then that at some time this would have to change, but I did
not *really* know it. Wishful thinking kept me supposing that
it was not really going to happen to me – or at least not in
the extreme way that it seemed always to happen in the
accounts I had read by missionaries and others who had
themselves lived "the life of faith". In those accounts the
saving cheque always arrives at the last possible moment
when disaster is at hand. I had optimistically calculated that
deliverance had to arrive around the 20th of September in
order to avert disaster. However, it appears that God's
standards of what constitutes "disaster" are on a different
scale from mine. Furthermore, it appears that His standards
are more accurate than mine, for in fact here I am almost a
month later, still with food and other necessities and with all
essential accounts paid. I don't know how much longer this
is going to go on. The encouraging part is that I am now
down to exactly 15p and my visitor's permit for staying in
the UK expires in less than a month. Thus I reassure myself
by telling myself that God's standards of disaster will shortly
be satisfied. I look forward eagerly to when that 15p will be
gone.'

Maynard Smith was horrified by this letter. He wrote immediately, offering financial help, and even rang with the same message, only for Price to tell him that things had not reached crisis point. He still had two cans of baked beans in the fridge – and his Barclaycard. The mention of the credit card persuaded Maynard Smith that there was little he could do to turn Price from his chosen course.

Despite the increasing fervour of his Tolstoyan Christianity, Price continued his scientific work while the rest of his life crumbled around him. The science was very successful. Immediately after announcing that he had only 15p left in the world, the letter quoted above took off into a discussion of a short paper that he and Maynard Smith were writing for *Nature*, the most important and prestigious scientific journal in the world. The two men had met because Price had in 1968 submitted to *Nature* an article on the theory of animal conflict. It had been sent on to Maynard Smith, a recognised authority, for his advice on whether it was worth publishing. This process of 'refereeing' is the essential quality-control mechanism of science. Reputable journals will only publish work which has been formally approved by other experts in the field in question – partly because no one editor of a general science journal can hope to understand all the fields it covers. The referees, who are usually anonymous, must vouch for the importance and quality of the discoveries claimed by a paper's author, so their role is crucial in forming the alliances, friendships, and occasional deep hatreds which map the social history of science. The paper that brought them together was far too long for *Nature* to publish, and as referee, Maynard Smith said so. But he also wrote to Price urging him either to submit a drastically cut version to *Nature* or to submit it at full length to the *Journal of*

Theoretical Biology, where he thought he could guarantee publication. Price, characteristically, did neither, and the paper was never published in its original form. Instead, he started his work on Hamilton's equations, and was soon collaborating with him.

Price came to biology as an amateur in 1967, when he was 44. He had trained as a chemist, working on uranium analysis for the Manhattan Project in his early twenties, and getting a doctorate in the subject from Harvard, where he taught for a couple of years. He did medical research at the University of Minnesota in the early Fifties, and then spent four years as a freelance journalist and technical writer, while trying to write a book about Cold War strategy. He then spent six years working for IBM in New York State before emigrating to London.[2] This final move followed his divorce from a devoutly Catholic wife, and surgery for a tumour on his thyroid which left him dependent on medication to supply the missing products of his thyroid gland for the rest of his life: in his last years he sometimes stopped taking this to see if God would arrange a miracle to keep him alive. God did; he finally had to kill himself by snipping his carotid artery with nail scissors.

'Sell all you have and give to the poor.' The derelicts he entertained stole from him and made scenes. He was forced to leave his comfortable flat, and ended up dossing on the floor of the lab at University College in Bloomsbury where he had worked for six years. Not even that lasted. An alcoholic whose wife he had tried to help started to harass him at the lab, and at last took to shouting at him from the street below. So he had to leave there, too, and descended

---

2 Details from his CV, quoted in Steven Frank, 'George Price's Contributions to Evolutionary Biology'.

by degrees to the squat in Tolmers Square, north of Euston station, where he killed himself.

In a CV drawn up in the autumn of 1974, he listed various accomplishments, his doctorate and positions; he had left University College, he said, because 'I felt that the sort of theoretical mathematical genetics I was doing wasn't very relevant to human problems and I wanted to change to economics.' The last entry read: 'Worked June 14th to August 17th as a night office cleaner for a contract cleaning firm. (This work was undertaken for reasons having something to do with Christianity. I was considered to be slow but unusually dependable, so that after a while the supervisor did not bother to inspect my work. Left because my reasons for wanting a night job no longer held.)'

The social geography of London packs a great deal of variety into an extremely small space, so that pockets of real squalor and deprivation are found amid the solid bourgeois terraces of Bloomsbury. He had moved only about a mile east from Marylebone, but it would be hard to fall further. His cremation was attended only by a few of the tramps he had helped – and by Maynard Smith and Hamilton, then almost unknown but now among the most revered and distinguished biologists in the world, thanks in large part to the work that they started in collaboration with Price.

The two men had not seen each other for years until Price's funeral. Hamilton for a while bore a grudge against Maynard Smith for – as he thought – belittling his work. Maynard Smith had been teaching at University College London in the late Fifties when Hamilton was a student there. He rebukes himself still for failing to recognise that Hamilton was special: 'Bill felt at that time that I was the one boy who should have understood his ideas – and I didn't, confronted with this totally inarticulate kid. I just failed to do what a teacher ought to do, which was to recognise genius in a student.'[3]

Hamilton believed for a while that his teacher had done more than ignore him. Maynard Smith had been the beloved disciple of J. B. S. Haldane, who was one of the men who showed that Darwinian evolution and Mendelian genetics were not (as biologists had believed in the early years of this century) contradictory, but instead meshed together to explain the living world beautifully. When he was finding letters from Price for me in his office at Sussex University, Maynard Smith happened on the last letter Haldane had written him, announcing his diagnosis of cancer, and forty years after receiving it wept with heartbreaking spontaneity. After Hamilton's equations had been published, Maynard Smith told the story of how Haldane used to answer the question 'Would you lay down your life for your brother?' with 'For two brothers, certainly, or four cousins.' This certainly contained the germ of a theory of kin selection, but it was Hamilton who did all the mathematical work in circumstances of overwhelming loneliness. Sometimes he wrote sitting on a bench in Waterloo station, just to avoid being alone in his bedsit. When he learnt that Maynard Smith was telling the story of Haldane's anecdote, he misunderstood this as an attempt to rob him of the credit. He was bitter and furious and wrote some savage letters. Price did his best to reconcile the two men, even though he was himself capable of quarrelling with each of them individually.

Yet this curious figure, intermittently insane and almost entirely misunderstood, who had managed to quarrel with or offend almost everyone who ever worked with him, and

---

3 Interview with the author. Hamilton and Maynard Smith are friends again now, by the way.

who was in death mocked even by his priest, had worked on three of the most influential scientific ideas of the late twentieth century. The application of game theory to animal behaviour, which he had worked on with Maynard Smith; the discussion of how co-operative behaviour could spread in a Darwinian world, which he worked on with Hamilton; and the general theory of selection, which would apply Darwinism to everything but which he never completed: these form a trilogy of ideas which have since his death become enormously powerful and fashionable. In thirty years they have gone from being heretical to being self-evident, even though their original expression is rigorously mathematical.

If your eye skids away from equations as though they were black ice on the page, or if you feel that *any* mathematical exercise is sufficient reason for suicide, relax. The broad truths they express can be much more simply put in English: what the equations provide is a way for biologists to make precise predictions from these insights, and to check them out in nature. But anyone interested in Price's equation can find it on the last page of this book.

It is not apparent to the non-mathematical reader why the discovery of Hamilton's equations should have driven anyone to suicide. None the less, the death of George Price followed in a fairly straight line from the breakdown he experienced as he came to terms with their meanings. What Price saw was that a world in which unselfishness really is rewarded can be even more horrible than one in which only the ruthless survive. The torment is that we want to be genuinely unselfish: gratuitously good. Humans are naturally idealistic and altruistic among many other, sometimes contradictory, things. Some part of everyone wants to make the leap that Jesus made in the parable of the Good Samaritan.

Yet our only test of whether we have succeeded in being good is our intuition, and this, if it is genetically produced and adaptive, can no longer be relied on. It is not a new dilemma. It applies as well to the difficulty of trusting our animal minds with metaphysical or mathematical speculation. But to a certain sort of temperament, the thing is unendurable.

The tormenting reflection is not that altruism is a con in the obvious, vulgar sense that it is 'really' selfish or that it 'really' advances our interests. Often it does not. It is impossible to interpret George Price's actions as advancing his interests, or even those of his genes, in any way at all. He was acting to the benefit of strangers, in a country far from his relatives, and in ways that could only diminish his status and bring him into danger. But this does not prove that natural selection could not have produced him, and all other idealists.

It is not necessary for altruistic acts to bring rewards to be genetically ordained. In fact, the imprecision of our urges towards selflessness, and the fact that they often really damage the altruist, are convincing evidence that they have been produced by Darwinian processes acting for the propagation of the genes that make them possible. The behaviours and dispositions produced by natural selection are always in some circumstances inadequate, inapposite or just plain wrong. We believe our eyes, and we rely on our hearts: yet we know that our eyes deceive us, and that our hearts fail us. These failures, metaphorical as well as physical, are evidence that these organs have evolved.

But our emotional constitution does more than direct us. It also orients us. It tells us what our goals are: wanting to behave well, or lovingly, is one of the things that tell us what good behaviour or love is. That is why it can seem so threatening that these desires have evolved fallibly, for if our wants and dispositions are as much a product of Darwinian forces as are our eyes, perhaps our instinct for what is goodness, or love will be as fallible as our eyesight. What is tormenting, then, is not just the idea that our acts are fundamentally selfish; it is the thought that our ideals are selfish, too.

The discovery that there might be a genetic basis for human idealism – which is what the equations amount to – appears to provide conclusive, final proof that all our best efforts are directed at illusions. For one thing, as Price saw clearly in extending the scope of the equations to cover 'spiteful' or 'selfish' behaviour, it showed that we could have evolved to be just as passionate about hatred and destruction as we are, most of the time, about construction. Indeed, some people clearly have done.

For William Hamilton, who originally discovered the equations, the horror of human selfishness seems the more urgent and important problem. 'It was the discussion of the darker of the "innate aptitudes" that I believed must exist in all human populations and most individual humans, and of the selection our forebears must have undergone through competition between populations, creating their warlike inclinations, including, perhaps, their relish in cruelty, that caused me most pain to write. . . . I believed that the violent and sadistic ideas, which seemed to arise so easily in my psyche in certain moods, must be vestiges from a period that occurred subsequent to the separation of the chimpanzee line',[4] that our vilenesses, in other words, are something distinctively human. For Hamilton, the Furies of Greek tragedy are the urges that allowed our hominid ancestors to torture their rivals and enjoy it. In an extraordinary passage in

---

4 *Narrow Roads of Gene Land*, p. 191.

his collected papers, he quotes, from Aeschylus' *Eumenides*,
Apollo's description of the Furies pursuing Orestes:

> *They fly, and do not weaken. They will hound you yet*
> *Through seas and island cities, over the vast continent,*
> *Wherever the earth's face is hard with wanderers' feet*

and adds that he wept when he first read it 'in a second hand
bookshop in central Sao Paulo in 1964. In the dark alcove
shut under the 20 teeming downtown storeys, applying the
passage to myself, I even cried: this was my relief, realising
how others had known my troubles so long before.'[5]

The peculiar horror is not that we are emotionally self-
interested: any fool can see that; but that it is our nature to
be intellectually deceived as well. A. E. Housman remarked
that the longing for truth was the weakest of all human
passions; Price's equation appears to show that we may very
well love truth, a little, but that even if we do, we would
have no way of knowing when we found it.

> *Books bear him up a while and make him try*
> *To swim with bladders of philosophy;*
> *In hopes still to o'ertake th'escaping light,*
> *The vapour dances in his dazzling sight,*
> *Till spent, it leaves him to eternal Night.*
> *Then Old Age, and Experience, hand in hand,*
> *Lead him to Death, and make him understand,*
> *After a search so painful, and so long,*
> *That all his life, he has been in the wrong.*
> *Huddled in dirt the reasoning engine lies,*
> *Who was so proud, so witty and so wise.*

---

5 Ibid.

This is of course an intuition that stands independently of Darwinism, and perhaps of modern science, but it is always painful: the man who wrote that 'Satire against Mankind', the Earl of Rochester, died in 1680, while Newton was alive. What Darwinism has added is a conviction that the outcome of the struggle can be predicted mathematically. It is the idea that both our good and our evil urges have a genetic component (and that the triumph of evil may be predicted by game theory) which gives Hamilton's thought its distinctive flavour of grand melancholy fatalism.

Since George Price's suicide, we have had to come to terms with a world in which all human endeavour seems an illusion, serving the purposes of brute genetic fact. In Penelope Lively's novel *City of the Mind* (1991), the hero reflects, 'There was the genetic drive, boiling away unsuspected while you got on with the rest of life, or at least you thought that that was what you were doing. The genes lurked there in the body, determining everything – whether you were six feet tall or prone to sunburn or liable to develop a particular disease – and quite possibly directing your actions as well.' Price's suicide shows that, if one really understands what this vision means, it can be overwhelming; but also, paradoxically, that it need not be; for everything about the drama of his breakdown and his recovery is pitched on a human scale, not in the grand, abstract landscapes of genetic fitness. Whatever made him kill himself at the vision of a world ruled by selfish genes, it was not his genes.

It was, perhaps, a vision of the world as mechanism. There are many ways of trying to understand the grip of Darwinism on our imaginations, but one of the simplest and most powerful facts about it is that it is beautiful, and to those who grasp it this beauty seems evidence also of its truth, and inexorability. It may be the greatest extension of mathematical beauty to the natural world since the Pythagoreans started to meditate on geometry. Geometry deals with patterns in space, and Darwinism with patterns in time. In both cases a deep order appears out of the confusion of the world, but the effect of this order can be curiously alienating. If the world is geometrical, where does that leave us, poor irregular creatures, unquenchably convinced we can square circles? And if the unfolding of history is similarly bound by mathematically expressible laws, where does that leave us and our freedom? These are not rhetorical questions: at least, they are questions to which it is possible to provide answers. But the answers are not obvious.

Part of the reason for this difficulty is religious, or irreligious. Preceding ages would have found nothing very strange or threatening in the idea that we are limited, determinate beings, if only because they devoted considerable resources to transcendent experience. They had another reason, just as powerful, of course, which is that for most of history no one would have taken seriously for a moment the idea that we are undetermined, existentialist beings, capable in principle of unlimited freedom. It was only in Western Europe and America, in the long, decompressing boom after the Second World War, that it really seemed for a while as if the sky were not the limit, and that we would leap from the moon, through the rest of the solar system, and out into the galaxy, as a matter of inevitability. In 1998, the world seems a much crueller and more limited place. We take it for granted that we will get richer and richer, but that this will not really make us happier. But in the period when Hamilton, Price, and Maynard Smith were first working out their ideas, it seemed that all these riches and all that freedom would have cash value, as philosophers say (meaning almost the opposite): they could be exchanged for happiness.

I am just old enough to remember that future: the first live television I remember seeing was the broadcast of Neil Armstrong on the moon, and later I lived for years in Sweden, one of the corners of Europe where the future lingered longest. Human nature then seemed as boundless as human potential. 'We, alone, can rebel against the tyranny of selfish replicators', as one slogan of the period went. This euphoria was not purely economic. There was also a religious, or moral, argument for optimism of this sort. Part of the collateral damage when God died was the loss of any firm connection between might and right. If constraints and suffering were no longer part of any divine plan, there was no reason to accept them; it sometimes seemed almost immoral, cowardly, to admit their existence. In biology there was the particular warning of the Nazis, whose enthusiastic understanding of the Darwinian nature of human life discredited for decades the idea that genetic constitution was what mattered about a human being, and so of a fixed human nature. Hamilton, when he started his research in the late Fifties at the LSE, found that any interest in eugenics was regarded with the deepest suspicion by his supervisors.

Years later, Hamilton wrote: '. . . all my own attempts to tell people that a principle of this kind was needed in biology and this was what I was working on were met by the sourest rebuffs – words to the effect that I was wasting my time, there was no such thing as genetic altruism, or at best total disinterest. I can remember persons telling me that everything that seemed worth doing on altruism had been done by [R. A.] Fisher and Haldane but when questioned as to where the work could be read I never found that they knew of anything other than what was in the books of 1930 and 1932, which of course I had read long ago.

'I suppose it is *understandable* that a disciple without a master must expect a hard time and that statements that seem significant or humorous according to the hearer's mood when uttered by a famous scientist seem to be heretical and ridiculous pretension when uttered by a detached graduate student, but I can't help feeling that it is wrong that this should be so in a university. But I also have in mind that I was a rather retiring kind of student who preferred to withdraw from people who found me ridiculous rather than argue back.'[6]

How the wheel turns! The LSE now, only forty years later, is the home of Darwin Seminars devoted to proving that Darwinian perspectives can explain almost everything in the world, and certainly everything in human nature. To a large proportion of intellectuals Darwinism has become what the philosopher Daniel Dennett calls 'a universal acid' which can eat through any of the problems which have defeated the best minds of all preceding generations. Darwin has been called in aid to explain almost everything about human beings from their shape and preference for copulating face to face to their tendency to depression and eating sweets. There are schools of Darwinian medicine; and of Darwinian psychology; but the new explanations do not stop with humans. There are books about Darwinian cybernetics. William Calvin, an American neuroscientist, has a Darwinian theory of how the brain works; and Gerald Edelman, a biochemist, another one. Edelman has already won a Nobel prize for showing how the immune system works by the Darwinian process of variation and selection. Then there are influential philosophers of science like David Hull who propose that science itself can be understood as a

---

6 Letter to John Maynard Smith, 23 October 1980.

process of varying and winnowing ideas; and even more influential general philosophers who seem to think that every human activity can be reduced to this paradigm.

In fact, anyone who reads this book has probably been swept up in the revolution themself: it has been the great intellectual excitement of the last twenty years. The only comparable source of new ideas and metaphors has been the world of computers. The two are connected. Though many of the founders of sociobiology are close and devoted observers of the animal world, to whom there is scarcely any higher term of praise than 'naturalist', all of them are mathematically literate and dependent on computers for the work they do. Price himself worked for IBM for six years, doing a mixture of programming and managing; his letters to Maynard Smith are full of references to the incidental inconveniences of computing in those days when all your programming was done on punched cards. When I went to see Hamilton at his office in Oxford, the first books I noticed on the shelves were not biological, but programming manuals.

The difference, however, is that computers provide tactical tools, not strategic plans. In the first rush of discovery and excitement when we start using them, it seems that everything in the world can be understood in terms of computer jargon. But the longer we use them, the clearer their limitations become. Darwinian thought is the opposite. The longer you use it, the more powerful a tool it seems, for understanding everything. Its limits emerge only gradually, intermittently, and for many people never come into focus.

None the less, there are limits to the value and use of Darwinian ideas. The struggle to establish these limits over the last thirty years forms the subject of this book. This is not an argument over their truth, or an account of difficulties with creationists. If one takes seriously the Christian promise that truth will prevail, then creationism will wither away; if one does not take the Bible as a reliable guide to the world, then creationism will never arise. The Darwin wars are not between believers and disbelievers in evolution, or in Darwinism. They are about the scope and proper limits of Darwinian explanations. All sides in these arguments take for granted that where there is design in nature, it has been produced by Darwinian processes operating for a long time in reasonably stable environments. The question in dispute is not 'where does design come from?' but 'where does it stop?'; and to some extent it is a question to which there can be no definite answer.

The oddest thing about all this excitement is that it is not a result of new observations. It started with a new way of looking at already known facts. Hamilton's equations did predict ways in which social behaviour might arise in some insects, on the basis of their peculiar arrangements for dividing chromosomes between the sexes, which mean that sisters are more closely related to each other than they are to their brothers or even their mothers: Hamilton predicted on this basis that the worker castes would always be females, and the males, among social insects, would always be drones. But most social behaviour arises among animals which share chromosomes and genes normally with their relatives. Hamilton's detailed reasoning about the social insects was exciting chiefly to entomologists.

One of these, a fiercely ambitious American named Ed Wilson, read Hamilton's 1963 paper on a long train ride from Boston, where he worked, to Florida, where the most interesting ants were found. Year later, he described the effect it had on him. 'My first response was negative. Impossible, I thought; this can't be right. Too simple. He must not know much about social insects. But the idea kept gnawing at me early that afternoon, as I changed over to the Silver Meteor in New York's Pennsylvania Station. As we departed southward across the New Jersey marshes, I went through the article again, more carefully this time, looking for the fatal flaw I believed must be there. At intervals I closed my eyes and tried to conceive of alternative, more convincing explanations of the prevalence of hymenopteran social life and the all-female worker force. Surely I knew enough to come up with something. I had done this kind of critique before and succeeded. But nothing presented itself now. By dinnertime, as the train rumbled on into Virginia, I was growing frustrated and angry. Hamilton, whoever he was, could not have cut the Gordian knot. Anyway, there was no Gordian knot in the first place, was there? I had thought there was probably just a lot of accidental evolution and wonderful natural history. And because I modestly thought of myself as the world authority on social insects, I also thought it unlikely that anyone else could explain their origin, certainly not in one clean stroke. The next morning, as we rolled on past Waycross and Jacksonville, I thrashed about some more. By the time we reached Miami, in the early afternoon, I gave up. I was a convert, and put myself in Hamilton's hands. I had undergone what historians of science call a paradigm shift.'[7]

Thirty years later, 'a paradigm shift' is a marketing term like everything else. But it still has a technical meaning within the philosophy of science, where it means one of those rare discoveries that change everything, and force the reassessment of all sorts of previously obvious theories. A paradigm is in some aspects similar to a myth: it provides the

---

7 Wilson, *Naturalist*, p. 319.

story and the assumptions into which our other discoveries are fitted; the light in which everything else is interpreted.

Wilson became one of the most enthusiastic and influential popularisers of the genetics of altruism, and a ferocious combatant in the Darwin wars.[8] Yet his story brings out the fact that the wars have been about changes in understanding, not sensational discoveries about the world. They have brought few new facts into light; what they have done is change the sort of facts that people find interesting and important.

The excitement has coincided with a shift in understanding, and in the relative prestige of different sciences. In popular culture, evolution and concepts drawn from evolutionary theory have become the kind of big juju words that 'radioactivity' and 'atomic' were earlier this century: in the 1920s, it was a selling point to call medicines 'radioactive'; and in the 1950s, 'atomic power' meant 'cheap, safe, and plentiful'. Now we have reached the stage where evolutionary biology crops up on *The X Files*, in which Scully tells Mulder that 'language, evolution, is a series of steps, not leaps' and Mulder replies: 'Recent evolutionary theory would disagree. What scientists call punctualism or punctual equilibrium. It theorises that evolutionary advances are cataclysmic, not gradual; that evolution occurs not along a straight graphable line, but in huge fits and starts. And that the unimaginable happens in between the gaps.'

Never mind that it is actually 'punctuated equilibrium' (or that the short form is 'punk eek'). Never mind that the theory says nothing of the sort (what Mulder is actually describing is the doctrine of saltationism). What is really extraordinary, and demands explanation, is how a theory

---

8 More on him in Chapter 3.

conceived among the trilobites in the American Museum of Natural History in New York to explain certain curious features of the fossil record should have found its way onto a television programme that depicts the myths we live by. The story of this revolution in popular culture is the story of this book.

2

THE BIRTH OF THE SELFISH GENE

THE IDEA OF the selfish gene can be traced back as far as William Hamilton's very first paper, 'The Genetical Evolution of Social Behaviour', written in 1963; but agency and intelligence did not appear among genes until 1972, when Hamilton was trying to dramatise and clarify his explanation for the evolution of sterile worker castes among the ants. 'A gene is being favoured in natural selection if the aggregate of its replicas forms an increasing fraction of the total gene pool', he wrote. 'We are going to be concerned with genes supposed to affect the social behaviour of their bearers, so let us try to make the argument more vivid by attributing to the genes, temporarily, intelligence, and a certain freedom of choice. Imagine that a gene is considering the problem of increasing the number of its replicas and imagine that it can choose between causing purely self-interested behaviour by its bearer A (leading to more reproduction by A) and causing "disinterested" behaviour that benefits in some way a relative, B. Specifically, let ∂A and ∂B represent the alternative increments to fitness that the gene in A is able to cause. Let the probability that our gene in A occurs as a replica in a random gamete of B be r_{AB}' – and so on for two paragraphs of mathematics, after which he surfaced briefly to write: 'We can now abandon the fanciful viewpoint of individual genes'[1] before plunging into the maths again. Seldom has so clever a man been so wrong. The mathematics are remembered by only a few professionals. The metaphor has run all round the world.

The book which spread that metaphor, *The Selfish Gene*, started as a course of lectures: Richard Dawkins is a wonderful teacher. He has two huge talents as a prophet of science: he can present explanations that intensify a sense of wonder at the world; and he can scythe through the lazy peripheral assumptions of common sense as if they were so many nettles. You can see this by comparing his books with those of the people whose ideas he shares. *The Selfish Gene* is largely an exposition and development of the ideas of Hamilton and John Maynard Smith: Hamilton has never tried to popularise his ideas, which leads to the peculiar Turkish bath quality of his collected papers, in which one is continually plunging from the warmth of the prefaces into the chilly mathematics of the papers themselves, before scrambling out to a fresh preface. Maynard Smith, by contrast, has written a popular textbook, *The Theory of Evolution*, which comes with a generous and enthusiastic foreword by Dawkins. It richly deserves this praise. It is beautifully lucid, scrupulous and clearly argued. But it is written on the assumption that the reader wants to learn. Dawkins, by contrast, writes as if what he has to say is overwhelmingly important to everyone, whether they want to learn or not. He expects the reader not just to be curious, but to be excited and delighted by what he will find.

I don't know anyone who has read his books and not come away fizzing with ideas. Some of them may be wrong

---

1 *Narrow Roads of Gene Land*, p. 273.

or ephemeral, but that is true of any author. And there are very few who can have succeeded as well as Dawkins does in opening up an entirely new way to ask questions about the world. More than any other author I know of, he makes vivid the central scientific idea that there are good logical reasons for things to happen one way rather than another and that we can, if we try, discover them.

This contagious enthusiasm is not to be explained by his genes, so let's tell a different sort of story, and say that when he was born in Nairobi in 1941 the fairies gathered round his cradle. The good fairy gave him good looks, intelligence, charm and a chair at Oxford specially endowed for him. The bad fairy studied him a while, and said: 'Give him a gift for metaphor.'

He has a talent for the dazzling phrase which would be remarkable in a professional writer. In a zoologist it appears a freak of nature. Two of his book titles, *The Selfish Gene* and *The Blind Watchmaker*, have entered the language and said farewell to their author as surely as Tennyson's 'Nature, red in tooth and claw'. But these phrases, like all great metaphors, dazzle as well as illuminate, and that is where the problem starts. Dawkins is controversial both as a scientist and as a philosopher of science and religion. Beneath the magnesium flaring of his metaphors, the world appears as bright islands of scientific enlightenment surrounded by a ravening darkness of ignorance and religion.

Yet Dawkins's brilliance as a controversialist is a large part of his appeal. He is one of those writers who cannot be comfortably read without a pen in hand: my copies of his books are covered in notes where the point of the biro has dug down into the paper: 'Balls!' and '!!', or long, tangled arguments that wander round all the margins of the page. By the time I met him, I felt I had been talking to him for years.

He is a neat, handsome, rather bird-like man, who pays attention to his plumage. In fact, this likeness goes deeper. When being interviewed, he has something of the quick distancing and self-possession of a bird. For a man of his success and fame he is surprisingly shy. This would not be odd in an Oxford lecturer in zoology, but it is, a little, in a *Wired* magazine pin-up.

He began his career as a student of Niko Tinbergen, who in 1973 shared a Nobel prize with Konrad Lorenz and Karl von Frisch for making respectable ethology, the science of animal behaviour. Lorenz, in 1937, was the first man to propose that an animal's intellectual equipment could be as much the subject of inheritance and selection as its physical characteristics are. Tinbergen had concentrated most of his efforts on birds; and one of his major discoveries was the way in which simple stimuli can lead to complex behaviours. One of the classic discoveries in this field, made by David Lack, a British ornithologist, was that a male robin will ignore a model robin – even if it is a perfectly stuffed male – if it has no red breast, but will attack ferociously a blob of red cloth on the end of a stick. One of the reasons this is important is that it is very much easier to imagine and to simulate a brain mechanism that recognises moving red patches in the environment, than it is to design 'robin-recognisers'. It is an example of the way in which complex behaviours can turn out to have simple causes: the desire to discover such relations, or to explain them, is fundamental to science: the question of how many causes you need to explain the behaviours of the world is also fundamental to the disputes within science about the reach and power of Darwinism.

In the late 1960s, Dawkins had taken some of Tinbergen's undergraduate lectures for him, when the professor was on sabbatical, and used the opportunity to plunge straight into the then important dispute about theories of group selection: 'I wanted to explain what was wrong with group selection and I wanted to go back, therefore, to the fundamentals of natural selection. It was at that point that I made up all the rhetoric of genes leaping down generations and casting bodies aside as they go. I used it again in my lectures in Berkeley, California, in the late Sixties; and then, when I returned to Oxford, I thought it would be a good idea to put it into a book.'[2]

The selfishness of genes consists in two qualities: they don't care what happens to us, their 'vehicles'; and they compete with each other to be reproduced. A cynic or even a mere realist might object at this point that *of course* they don't care about us: a microscopic string of goo can no more be selfish than it can be musical, and this is a point on which there were later to be acrimonious quarrels. Similarly, the point about genes competing with each other is less clear-cut than it can at first appear. Alternate forms of the same gene, alleles as they are known, can obviously be thought of as competing with each other. But that is because they are different possible conformations of the same stretch of chromosome.

Since genes cannot, by definition, really care, let us re-phrase the point about their selfishness: they cause to happen things which are enormously painful for their bearers: not merely some diseases, but death itself and much of the preceding decay are necessary for the Darwinian process to continue.

There is worse: at the same time as the process generates old age and every other form of frailty, it also tends to

---

2 Interview with the author, 1995.

increase the distress we feel in consequence. One of the most difficult natural phenomena to explain in Darwinian terms is the well-attested fact that people very close to death will often come into a sudden peace, whether being chewed by a lion or simply dying of exhaustion. I used to wonder for hours how such a thing could have evolved when it was so clearly for the benefit of the dying person and not of their descendants. A throwaway remark of Hamilton's supplies the answer: it is not the anaesthesia which has evolved, but its opposite: the capacity to feel pain. In some extreme circumstances when it is no longer useful to feel pain, we stop feeling it.[3] Normally, and certainly while an animal is capable of breeding, such a capacity will lead it to avoid whatever is painful. If agony promotes in it a lifesaving effort, then the capacity for agony will be passed on to its descendants (other things being equal). Only if agony actually reduces an animal's chance of breeding successfully will there be any selective pressure to diminish it, and most horrible deaths from disease are not of this sort.

Natural selection has produced not only suffering but cruelty, the relish we can take in cruelty and even the capacity to understand that there are such things as suffering and cruelty and that these are wrong.

For the moment, though, it is important to note that the 'selfishness' of Richard Dawkins's genes emphatically does not consist in the idea that they are genes for selfishness, though that is how most people seem to read it: the phrase elides, in shorthand, into genetic determinism and a rather Hobbesian view of the world. In popular usage 'a selfish gene' seems to mean something like 'a little brick of selfishness out of which we are made by sticking lots of them

---

3 Doesn't help much with cancer, though.

together until you get a big complicated edifice of selfishness, which is us'. This really was not what Dawkins was trying to say, though some of his language did suggest this meaning powerfully: 'The gene is the basic unit of selfishness' is one characteristic throwaway line in *The Selfish Gene* (p. 36).

In so far as *The Selfish Gene* was a popularisation of the ideas that Hamilton and Price had expressed in their equations for altruism, it could be read as a demonstration of how genuinely unselfish and co-operative behaviours can survive and flourish in a Darwinian world. Of course this co-operation may be hostile to some third party. When a bee stings you on the nose and dies, you do not immediately apprehend her act as altruistic.[4] When a doctor gives his life fighting a cholera epidemic, when he could leave the slum for a place of safety, this is genuinely altruistic in the sense that he is consciously and deliberately putting the welfare of other humans above his own (and that of his genes), even though he operates to the disadvantage of the cholera bacteria. The point about our 'selfish' genes is that they make us genuinely affectionate towards our kin, sociably disposed towards others, and on occasion really altruistic. One moral of *The Selfish Gene* is that genes, in fact, make us want to be good.

They don't, however, make us act well. Dawkins believed genes 'make' people in the sense of creating them, but do not 'make' people in the sense of compelling them. This was another important distinction that was rapidly lost. The

---

4 This facet of altruism is perhaps especially obvious to the entomologists who must collect altruistic insects. Hamilton reproduces a photograph of a Brazilian wasps' nest so fiercely defended that even though he approached it wearing full bee-keeper's garb he was incapacitated for two days.

German publishers of *The Selfish Gene* put on the cover of the first edition a picture of a human puppet jerking on the end of strings descending from the word 'Gen' (gene); and the French publishers a picture of bowler-hatted clockwork men with wind-up keys sticking out of their backs. This is not what Dawkins thought he meant at all. He had both covers changed, and lectured for a while using slides of the originals as illustrations of what he did not mean about genes.

But when you ask what it is that he did in fact mean about genes, you may well come away confused. I believe that this confusion can be cleared up, with sufficient application. But it is not unimportant or even, in a sense, accidental: the Darwin wars have been conducted like musketry battles, beneath huge clouds of smoke which thicken every time each side discharges its weapons until the entire battlefield is lost from view. If all the smoke and shouts and rhetoric were swept away, there would be very little disagreement about what genes are or how they affect the world: there is not complete agreement, but the disagreements are subtle, and take some time to reach.

The real Furies are not scientific, but philosophical, political, and sometimes personal. I have said before that *The Selfish Gene* is a book about genes that was read as a book about people. But this is true of all the popular science of the Darwin wars. Genes don't buy books: people do; and though the book-buying public may be interested in genes, successful publishers act on the principle that the public is really trying to maximise its knowledge about people.

This is a pity. Genes are actually fascinating even when we don't take them as divinities; and one of the most fascinating things about a gene-centred view of the world is how complex and subtle is the relationship between a gene and its environment.

There are two tricksy questions that haunt the discussion: 'What are genes for?' and 'How many genes make one?' If the first question is asked about genes in general, it becomes the question 'Why is there life in the universe?' to which there seems to be no satisfactory answer and which may not even be a question we can coherently ask. But you can always ask what a particular string of DNA is for, and hope for a coherent answer. Such an answer must say both what the immediate chemical effect of the gene is, and how this minute chemical effect fits into a causal chain which makes it likely that this pattern of DNA will be copied into fresh bodies. It must, in other words, explain how the string of DNA can be understood both by the molecular biologist and the population geneticist, both as a functional and as an analytical gene.

These answers can be complicated, but they have been found, at least for some bits of DNA. For instance, in humans, at location 11p15.5 on chromosome 11 there is a length of DNA which specifies a protein called β haemoglobin. To be more precise, it codes for a particular string of 146 amino acids: each string, once assembled, twists round itself and scrunchles up into the particular distinctive shape that makes it β haemoglobin. But it does not then float freely round the cell: instead, two of these proteins come together with two other, slightly different scrunchled molecules known as α haemoglobin, and the four parts fit together to make a single, huge molecule which has in the middle of its complicated shape a cavity in which an oxygen molecule can nestle. So that is what the gene does from the point of view of the molecular biologist.

That is half the answer to the question of what this particular gene is. It is certainly very odd, but it may seem more odd than interesting, until you realise that if this process stops you die. It provides the chemical mechanism which makes blood useful. The chief purpose of blood is to transport oxygen round the body, and it is the haemoglobin that makes this possible: it carries oxygen round the body to where it is needed, molecule by molecule, and then – just as importantly – releases the oxygen molecules there. And all this convoluted chain of consequences follows logically from the order in which the bases in one small fragment of DNA are arranged. Knowing that, we can see why it is selected and what purpose it serves, which is the sort of answer a geneticist might look for.

So it looks as if we have got a completely satisfying answer to the question 'What is this gene found at such and such a location on chromosome tiddlysquit?' It makes a protein which makes most animal life possible. It is a gene for making a vital part of blood. This explanation links the functional gene with the analytical gene. We seem to have got it all.

The trouble is that these two explanations are not rigidly fixed to each other. Other genes can produce haemoglobin. Human foetuses have a different form of haemoglobin, which is slightly more efficient at attracting oxygen molecules than the adult sort. Babies in the womb have two slightly shorter crumpled strings, called γ haemoglobin, fitted in to the big haemoglobin molecule where the adult version has β haemoglobin proteins. This γ haemoglobin is produced by the instructions in a different piece of DNA to that which produces the β sort: which one gets used is determined by other genes which switch them on or off.

But the string of DNA which normally produces β haemoglobin comes in two different forms, or alleles. One allele, different only by one very small change, produces S haemoglobin, a protein that works almost the same way as the β sort. It takes up oxygen, transports it round the body, and releases it – but then it does not snap back to its normal shape. Instead, it straightens out, and forms bundles with other molecules of the same sort, and these get so large that they distort the red blood cells containing them, pushing them into a stiff curved shape, like a sickle. At this point, the DNA that specifies S haemoglobin has become a gene for dying rather horribly. The sickle-shaped red blood cells jam in the smaller blood vessels, which cuts off the flow of blood, and hence of oxygen, beyond them. This destruction can be extraordinarily painful: anyone so afflicted also suffers from shortness of breath, chronic anaemia, and fever, and usually dies in childhood.

Yet this horrible, debilitating disease is so common in some populations that it must be maintained there by natural selection. The gene that produces it is found in as many as 40 per cent of the population in parts of West Africa. It turns out that this S haemoglobin goes rigid and forces cells sickle-shaped not just when it gives up its oxygen molecule, but also in the presence of the malaria parasite. Since the fate of a sickled cell is to wedge against the wall of a blood vessel and be destroyed, any malaria parasites inside are destroyed with it. So it turns out that S haemoglobin is in small quantities a protection against malaria, though it kills you if it is the only sort you have.

You have two copies of the string of DNA that makes haemoglobin, one from each parent. If the relevant part of both make S haemoglobin, you will probably die young from sickle-cell anaemia if nothing else carries you away first. If both make normal β haemoglobin, you are at risk from malaria, a disease that is very common and often fatal. But if some of your copies of the gene make malaria-resistant S haemoglobin, and the others make oxygen-carrying β

haemoglobin, you will be resistant to malaria without being anaemic.

The gene for S haemoglobin is maintained in the population in West Africa because the people who have only one copy of it will on average live longer and have more children than those who have either none or two copies. If two parents in a malarial region each have only one copy of the gene, and are therefore malaria-resistant without being anaemic, and they have four children, on average, one child will draw two copies of the S gene from the genetic shuffle and die in childhood; one will draw no copies, and die of malaria, probably in childhood too. The other two will draw the winning hand and survive to have children of their own – who will face the same odds at conception.

This is a dramatic simplification of the real process, but it illustrates the underlying logic of natural selection clearly enough. And the story of sickle-cell anaemia is usually told to illustrate this logic, or what Charles Darwin called 'the clumsy, wasteful, blundering, low, and horridly cruel works of nature'.[5] But there is another moral that can be drawn from it, and this is that the meaning of a gene, what it is 'for', is in important ways not specified by the DNA it is made of. Exactly the same stretch of DNA in exactly the same person can be a gene 'for' anaemia, for malaria resistance, or even for both. It all depends on which other genes it shares a body with, and where that body is. So the meaning of genes is not something in their nature, but something that emerges (like the meaning of words) from their interactions with the outside world and with each other.

Genes speak a language, not a code. This difference in metaphor reflects a hugely important fact about the way

---

5 Letter to J. D. Hooker, 13 July 1856.

genes influence bodies. With a code, the link between two meanings is rigid: with a language, it is flexible and context-dependent in all sorts of ways.

This is one of those truths which are so obvious to geneticists that sometimes they become invisible to them, too. You can only tell what a gene is 'for' if you look at it in context. This is a point that Richard Dawkins made over and over again in the earlier part of his career. 'If I have . . . [two copies of] a gene G, nothing save mutation can prevent my passing G on to all my children. So much is inexorable. But whether or not I, or my children, show the phenotypic effect normally associated with possession of G may depend very much on how we are brought up, what diet or education we experience, and what other genes we happen to possess. So, of the two effects that genes have on the world – manufacturing copies of themselves, and influencing phenotypes – the first is inflexible apart from the rare possibility of mutation; the second may be exceedingly flexible', he wrote in *The Extended Phenotype* (p. 14); and again, discussing the vexed question of whether there are, or could be, genes for homosexuality: 'What does it *mean* to say there is a genetic component to the difference, in common parlance that there is a gene (or genes) "for" homosexuality? . . . A gene "for" A in environment X may well turn out to be a gene for B in environment Y. It is simply meaningless to speak of an absolute, context-free, phenotypic effect of a given gene' (p. 38).

He seems to have been genuinely shocked that sociobiology upset women by predicting that temperamental sex differences are innate. Suppose being a man – possessing a Y chromosome – did have an influence on musical ability, or fondness for knitting, he asks, what would this mean? Only that, 'in some specified population and in some specified environment, an observer in possession of information about an individual's sex would be able to make a statistically more accurate prediction as to the person's musical ability than an observer ignorant of the person's sex. The emphasis is on the word "statistically", and let us throw in an "other things being equal" for good measure. The observer might be provided with some additional information, say on the person's education or upbringing, which would lead him to revise, or even reverse, his prediction based on sex. If females are statistically more likely than males to enjoy knitting, this does not mean that all females enjoy knitting, nor even that a majority do' (p. 12).

This is an awful long way from his more famous assertion that 'genes created us, body and mind'. There is a way round this contradiction, though. Just as Dawkins uses the language of selfishness and altruism in a technical biological sense rather than in its everyday sense which has something to do with moral philosophy, so, too, he talks about humans like biologists, but still using the language that non-biologists do. We take references to 'humans' or to 'us' to be references to individuals. Dawkins – at least part of the time – tends to treat them as references to characteristics of the species being worked on by natural selection. That is perhaps the way that a population biologist must study his own species. This characteristic is still clearer in the prefaces to William Hamilton's collected papers, where vivid personal recollections flash down from a grand melancholy fatalism. 'I am a child of the receding wave of the Romantic Movement, and as such I still hanker for miracles', he wrote, when discussing the difference between human and biological altruism, and how it has seemed all his life to narrow, until only 'miracles' can preserve the special qualities we intuit about human altruism.

Hamilton's further speculations bring one back to the world of Olaf Stapledon, an early, towering writer of science fiction[6] whose *Last and First Men* dealt with successive mutations of the human race (there were twenty-five or twenty-six species in all) over hundreds of thousands of years. It seems to Hamilton that if, in a nuclear and industrialised age, the human race is to survive, it must adapt itself drastically. 'For me, either it is eugenics, or else, not many generations hence, tranquillisers and other mood drugs and unlimited medical patches for every one of us all the time, combined with general submission to the idea that being no longer capable of free life we are destined, as individuals, to submerge indefinitely, to take status as mere executive cells within superorganisms that are forming around us and which we serve.

'Our controllers if this happens will be simply the civilised systems already established, although I foresee hospitals becoming much larger and more prominent components. In effect these will become major centres of the immune system of the superorganisms and they will also make up for the growing medical incompetence of individual "cells" – that is, us. Mass media will simulate the endocrines, networked computers and telephones merge to become our controlling nervous system, and computers will double again through their attachment to huge data bases of knowledge that increasingly only they "understand", to link together the "superbrains" controlling all that we do. . . . People will still feel themselves to be independent but actually will be entering increasing dependence on each other, on interactions with their machines (especially those for communication,

---

6 He is also admired by George Williams, who fixed the usage of 'gene' as a unit of heredity.

computation, and information retrieval), and on support from outside (e.g. from still relatively healthy manual workers and traditional hardware).

'In this general direction there certainly can be and has begun a viable programme. However, it must not be imagined that the harshness of natural selection can ultimately be evaded by this route. In addition to what a superbrain might decide to be proper economy within its own "body", there will eventually begin to be nasty die offs of whole systems as superorganisms themselves have to compete.'[7]

One sees in this extraordinary passage the blending of evolutionary theory with science fiction – in this case E. M. Forster's short story 'The Machine Stops', as well as Olaf Stapledon.

From the viewpoint of the gene, which Dawkins strives to attain, individuals have already disappeared. The problem is not that individuals are short-lived, but that they differ so much from generation to generation. The particular arrangement of DNA in any given human is probably unique. It certainly will not replicate itself often enough or faithfully enough to be selected.

Genes at least, Dawkins says, live long enough to matter. They are not immortal: they are simply very long lived by comparison with bodies. "A gene is . . . any portion of chromosomal material which potentially lasts for enough generations to serve as a unit of natural selection . . . [it is] a chunk of chromosomal material which, in practice, behaves as a unit for long enough to be naturally selected at the expense of another such fuzzy unit.'[8]

7 *Narrow Roads of Gene Land*, pp. 193–4.
8 'In Defence of Selfish Genes', p. 568, partly quoting from *The Selfish Gene*.

The Selfish Fuzzy Chromosomal Unit lacks something as a title but it might have avoided a lot of misunderstanding. For if you ask yourself why people nowadays believe in genes the way the ancient Greeks believed in Gods, and why they believe that human behaviour is determined by genes for everything, an idea which Dawkins has described as 'nonsense on an almost astrological scale', one answer is that they got these ideas from reading Richard Dawkins. Probably the best-remembered rhetoric in *The Selfish Gene* is a stirring invocation of the eternal gene: 'Now they swarm in huge colonies, safe inside gigantic lumbering robots, sealed off from the outside world, communicating with it by tortuous indirect routes, manipulating it by remote control. They are in you and in me; they created us, body and mind; and their preservation is the ultimate rationale for our existence. They have come a long way, those replicators. Now they go by the names of genes, and we are their survival machines' (pp. 19–20).

He has defended this metaphor twice, and at considerable length. This is in a way a pity, because the whole force of the passage derives from its lack of qualification, the way in which he launches himself, insouciant as a hang-glider, into great giddying updraughts of rhetoric. If he came to a bad end, as hang-gliders tend to, the last thing to do would be to try and repeat the flight, to prove he was in control all along. However, Dawkins is not a man to whom the words 'I was wrong' come easily.

A long note to Chapter 2 in the second edition of *The Selfish Gene* complains that 'This purple passage (a rare – well, fairly rare – indulgence) has been quoted and requoted in gleeful evidence of my rabid "genetic determinism". Part of the problem lies with the popular, but erroneous, associations of the word "robot" ' (p. 270).

This lofty condescension – 'popular, but erroneous' – is difficult for a popular writer to maintain. Who is he to tell us what the erroneous associations of the word 'robot' are? The answer is that he, like Hamilton, has an imagination informed by science fiction. The note continues: 'We are in the golden age of electronics, and robots are no longer rigidly inflexible morons but are capable of learning, intelligence, and creativity. Ironically, even as long ago as 1920 when Karel Capek coined the word, "robots" were mechanical beings that ended up with human feelings, like falling in love.'

Dawkins's nerdy enthusiasms have got the better of him here: if your definition of 'robot' comes from Asimov and Karel Capek, then of course robots are capable of feelings and emotions. But Asimov and Capek wrote science fiction, which has the great merit of being neither science nor fact. In the real world – and certainly when he wrote that passage – robots were not just completely determined, but completely predictable, too. In 1998, it is possible to build robots whose behaviour is not completely predictable; it is even possible, though more difficult, to build robots whose unpredictability is kept within useful bounds. But none has carried this independence of mind to the extent of falling in love, or experiencing any other emotion. Some of the most sophisticated robot software in the world is COG, found in the artificial intelligence lab at MIT. It cannot move around yet: it sits on a pedestal and moves an arm. One AI researcher who was taken to see it on a Sunday, when it was all switched off and dark, told me he had caught himself feeling sorry for the machine when he left its room. He did not suggest it was feeling sorry for itself.

The man who told me this story, Mark Humphrys, believes, I think, that it will one day be possible to produce 'robots' which are sufficiently sophisticated to appear to have emotions. Indeed, as an undergraduate, he carried out one of the funniest experiments ever performed in computer science to prove his point, when he wrote a program that persuaded an American undergraduate to discuss his sex life in embarrassing detail, under the impression he was talking to another student. You may not think it is much of an intellectual challenge to persuade a computer-science student at a Midwestern university to tell a complete stranger when he last got laid; but it is a small milestone in human history to have produced a machine that can do this. It did not require his program to have emotions, creativity, or anything of the sort. It was Humphrys who once said that anyone worried about artificial intelligence should watch a robot football tournament, where he will learn that every match is decided by own goals.

But Dawkins, having picked up his definition of 'robot' as something capable of 'learning, intelligence, creativity', runs wildly away with it. He goes on to say in that note: 'If, like most of the critics of my "lumbering robot" passage, you are not religious, then face up to the following question. What on earth do you think you are, if not a robot, albeit a very complicated one?' (pp. 270–1). This may be meant as a rhetorical question, but it has a perfectly good philosophical answer anyway.

Just as quantity alters quality, so does complication. Every educated person – even Catholic theologians – now believes that the properties of our bodies and minds are scientifically explicable, and that we are built up from things obeying the ordinary laws of physics and chemistry in a predictable fashion. In that sense, of course we are all 'very complicated robots'. But it is almost the least interesting thing about us because the complication of us has been carried to the point where we follow complicated patterns of motivation in unpredictable ways. If, despairing of ever finishing this book, I were to jump off Beachy Head, the laws of physics may predict inexorably that I will hit the ground in a little less than six seconds. They won't and can't say anything about why I jumped, even though the decision was made entirely in accordance with them. This is a point which Dawkins himself clearly understands and makes in other contexts: we have to be careful to analyse things at the proper level of complication. But he loses all restraint as soon as he drifts into metaphysics. Nothing but the crudest imaginable division between 'matter' and 'spirit' will do for him there.

If mind does turn out to be a special case of mechanism, we have very little idea how it arises, and we will have to modify considerably our idea of what 'mechanism' means. That day may yet come: in fact I believe it is inevitable. But in the meantime, there is a well-understood sense of robot, or machine, which is something rigid, mechanical, and predictable. If I say of someone 'He walks like a robot', it is perfectly and completely clear what I mean: he moves something like one of the Walkers in *Star Wars*. And that is the second thing to object to about this famous passage. Of all the possible senses of 'robot', it is exactly the mechanical, clumsy, inanimate sense which comes to mind when Dawkins compares bodies or 'lumbering robots' with genes. This is an effect of the verbs he uses. Genes, he says in this passage, *use* techniques and artifices to ensure their own continuation; *swarm* in huge colonies; *manipulate* the world by remote control; *communicate* with it. They can even *give up a cavalier freedom*. And it is these active, nimble, sophisticated beings which Dawkins chooses to contrast with the 'robots . . . survival machines' they have 'created for their preservation' – who are us. Is it any wonder that people have understood his message as genetic determinism? Or is it surprising that critics have misquoted him as saying that genes 'control us' body and mind, and not that they have 'created us'. The distinction between control and create is real, and no doubt very vivid to Dawkins, but all of the imagery of this famous passage works to obliterate it.

There are few more powerful antidotes to vulgar Dawkins than thoughtful Dawkins. Yet vulgar Dawkins is undoubtedly what the market wants, and what it has, increasingly, been getting: 'DNA neither knows nor cares. DNA just is. And we dance to music',[9] he proclaimed in *River out of Eden*. Even when he does not talk as if genes were gods, Olympian dispensers of fate, he still uses verbs to suggest they are agents or spirits, manipulating the passive flesh around them. In *The Extended Phenotype* (p. 159), he urged that readers should 'deeply imbibe the fundamental truth that an organism is a tool of DNA rather than the other way around'. I think that all he means by this is that DNA is not a tool of the organism, which is true; but it does not follow from this truth that the organism must be a tool of DNA: the relationship may not be one of tool and user at all.

Of course it's possible that I'm wrong, and that he really does mean what he says, but in that case all the talk about resisting genetic determinism is just hot air. It's always hard to tell, when words, in his hands, mean more or less what he wants them to. He made his name proclaiming the selfishness of genes, but when this view was challenged he explained that successful 'selfishness' consisted largely in their capacity to co-operate with each other.[10] One defence

---

9 So they can be musical as well as selfish.

10 See *The Extended Phenotype*, p. 239: 'genes are correctly understood as being selected *for their capacity to co-operate* with other genes in the gene pool'.

of this flexibility of meaning is to say that a word is only a tool that a scientist may use as he chooses: but a word is a special sort of tool like a two-man saw, which works only if both parties to a conversation grasp it. It is no use waving it in the air and expecting the tree to fall down.

Many people, of course, did grasp what Dawkins meant. They may have been a minority among his readers, but they were a smart and influential minority. They have been sawing away at almost every problem in sight for years now.

3

MACHIAVELLI AMONG THE ENTOMOLOGISTS

As the ideas that Hamilton, Price, and Maynard Smith had worked out and that Dawkins had synthesised grew in popularity, it seemed that you could examine the whole of nature and find purpose there. Not any overriding purpose, to be sure, and not a very edifying one. 'Ideas of vaguely benevolent mutual co-operation are replaced by an expectation of stark, ruthless, opportunistic mutual exploitation.'[1] But at least a coherent unifying principle: the things you find in a Darwinian world will have Darwinian purposes. They will be there because they are adaptations. Their qualities will have been selected.

Starting in the late Seventies, there followed a sort of Cambrian explosion of adaptive explanations, radiating to answer every possible question. The wilder reaches of adaptationist thinking – those where we lack any clear idea of what is being selected, and which forces are selecting – have only gradually emerged and are still being explored. Some of the original ideas, like their Cambrian counterparts, were so strange they died out quickly. Others seemed at the time to make perfect sense, and to be about measurable

---

1 Dawkins, *The Extended Phenotype*, p. 55.

things. The most lasting and influential of these was human sociobiology.

Sociobiology was understood by some of its practitioners to be a science of animal behaviour, with no application to human beings at all.[2] But from 1975, when the book was published that made the word famous, there were people who saw it as applying to mankind as well and *Sociobiology* itself had nothing controversial in it about animals. It was people who caused the trouble.

The author was Ed Wilson, the driven Harvard entomologist who had been converted to Hamilton's theories on a long train ride to Florida. When Wilson was a child in Florida, he put his right eye out on a fish. It was the summer his parents split up, and he was fishing off the end of a pier when a small spined minnow he hoiked into the air flew into his eye. 'The pain was excruciating and I suffered for hours. But, being anxious to stay outdoors, I didn't complain very much. I continued fishing.' The pain went away after a few days, but a couple of months later he developed a traumatic cataract in that eye and had to have the lens removed in a barbarous operation, anaesthetised by dripping ether. The resulting damaged sight, which retained its acuity only at close range, led him to concentrate his studies on insects.

Full of enthusiasm, hard work, and a peculiarly American romanticism, Wilson had become an associate professor at Harvard at the age of 26, younger even than Jim Watson, the co-discoverer of DNA, whom he loathed. In the early Sixties, Watson and his fellow molecular biologists were confident that all biology would soon be reduced to molecular biology: they had discovered what genes were

---

2 Matt Ridley, e-mail to the author, 19 March 1998.

made of, and the rest of the living world could all be worked out from the implications of this discovery. He did not mellow much with age: 'There is only one science, physics: everything else is social work,' Watson said[3] after he had become director of the Human Genome Project.[4]

One might think that the threat to science comes from the ignorant, the religious, and the obscurantist. And sometimes it does. But often the real threat to the survival of any academic discipline is other academics who are competing for the same pot of money and prestige: in the early Sixties, biologists did not feel nearly so threatened by creationists as by their molecular colleagues. In this highly pressurised atmosphere, when the traditional biologists at Harvard were meeting regularly to establish the independence of their discipline, Wilson came across Hamilton's original paper, in which the equations for altruism were first laid out, and was overwhelmed. He saw that it revolutionised his own discipline. He began to hope that it could revolutionise others.[5]

After he had finished a monumental study of the social insects in 1971, summarising everything that was known about them for the benefit of fellow academics, he turned his mind to the wider world. He set out to write a book that would bring all the patterns of social behaviour among animals under one cover, and show that these, where they were interesting, were genetically based and adaptive. Since people are also animals, this would incidentally solve a lot of

---

3 To Steven Rose, at the 1994 Cheltenham Literary Festival.

4 This is the immensely ambitious (and expensive) project of listing and mapping the entire sequence of DNA in human chromosomes, working out which bits are genes and, ultimately, working out what each gene does.

5 This process is described both in Wilson's autobiography, *Naturalist*, and, less dramatically, in David Hull's *Science as a Process*.

puzzles about human nature. The conscious scope and ambition of the plan was remarkable. Its unconscious assumption that the problems of human behaviour could all be sorted out with a little scientific rigour is more remarkable still: there is a principle known as Conquest's law which states that everyone is a reactionary about the subjects he understands.[6] The career of Ed Wilson brings out a corollary to this principle: that everyone is a reductionist about subjects that they don't understand.

Reductionism was originally the idea that complicated phenomena can be understood in terms of more simple and fundamental causes: as such it is an enormously powerful insight responsible for most of the triumphs of science over the last four hundred years. But it is a hope or an aspiration as much as an accomplishment: we cannot actually yet condense all the world's workings to a set of first principles and their outworkings. This may be because we don't yet know how to do it; the chain of causation is simply too long to get reliably from the Big Bang, which is a matter of simple physics, to the physicists who study it, and who must in turn be studied using biology, philosophy, chemistry, and other disciplines. Or it may be impossible in principle to get from physics to philosophy.

Whichever is the case, there are always things that any particular science can't explain, and so 'reductionist' has become both a productive way to ask questions of the world, and a term of abuse to describe people who think they've found all the answers. Every scientist understands quite well why his own discipline cannot be completely reduced to any other: chemists know that they are not just doing physics

---

6 Named by and after Robert Conquest, poet and distinguished historian of Stalinism.

with knobs on; biologists understand that there is more to the behaviour of living creatures than their chemical composition; historians know that history is more than the sum of biographies, and so on. (Philosophers are a limiting case in this rule, since they understand that *all* scientists are only doing more or less inadequate philosophy.) But many scientists suppose that anyone in the university who is doing work inessential to their own field could have their discipline, and department, productively reduced.

Wilson announced in 1975 that all the social sciences would have to be boiled down to biology before being reconstituted. His confidence that the study of humanity could be reconstructed on a basis drawn from population biology shocked philosophers quite as much as the particular characteristics were shocking, too: a book of similar ambition to *Sociobiology*, which, however, fizzled out almost unremarked, had been published the year before by one of Wilson's Harvard colleagues, the philosopher Michael Ghiselin.[7] It contained one of the most notorious passages of sociobiological rhetoric:

No hint of genuine charity ameliorates our vision of society, once sentimentalism has been laid aside. What passes for cooperation turns out to be a mixture of opportunism and exploitation. The impulses that lead one animal to sacrifice himself for another turn out to have their ultimate rationale in gaining advantage over a third; and acts 'for the good' of one society turn out to be performed to the detriment of the rest. Where it is in his interest, every organism may reasonably be expected to aid his fellows. Where he has no alternative, he submits to

---

7 *The Economy of Nature and the Evolution of Sex.*

the yoke of communal servitude. Yet given a full chance to act in his own interest, nothing but expediency will restrain him from brutalizing, from maiming, from murdering – his brother, his mate, his parent, or his child. Scratch an 'altruist,' and watch a 'hypocrite' bleed.[8]

This may be nasty, but it is not new. Compare it with another analysis of human nature: 'Men are ungrateful, fickle, simulators and deceivers, avoiders of danger, greedy for gain; and while you work for their good they are completely yours, offering you their blood, their property, their lives, and their sons, when danger is far away; but when it comes nearer to you they turn away. . . . They are less hesitant about harming someone who makes himself loved than one who makes himself feared because love is held together by a chain of obligation which, since men are wretched creatures, is broken on every occasion in which their own interests are concerned; but fear is sustained by a dread of punishment which will never abandon you' – but that was Niccolò Machiavelli, writing in 1513.[9]

The controversies over sociobiology which constitute the major part of the Darwin wars involved two interlocking questions: is human nature really as Machiavelli described it? And, if it is, does this follow inexorably from our genes? The first objection is one that has only slowly gained force. The example of George Price in his selfless last years shows clearly that human nature need not be like that. But there were few counter-examples as inspiring in the controversies which followed the publication of *Sociobiology* and which centred around the second question: how much of our

---

8 Quoted in Hull, *Science as a Process*, p. 226.
9 *The Prince*, Chapter 17 (p. 56).

character can be read out from our genes?

Ghiselin was consistent in his view of human nature: when the manuscript was delayed in press, he suspected that the referees were not only ideological opponents, such as Stephen Jay Gould, but sympathisers such as Wilson, and Robert Trivers, a manic-depressive biologist who had worked on the applications of game theory to animal behaviour at the same time as Maynard Smith, but independently.[10]

Trivers produced another of the founding ideas of sociobiology, the theory of reciprocal altruism. As usual, the new meaning of the phrase breaks the old skins of the words: human altruism is by definition not reciprocated. When George Price tried to help his tramps and outcasts, they stole from him and in one case drove him from the laboratory on whose floor he was sleeping until he was chased into the squat where he died. Reciprocal altruism, by contrast, is a pattern that emerges over generations and requires no emotion at all. It is an explanation for the way in which the emotions that make us genuinely altruistic might have evolved.

One of the classic examples comes from fish, animals whose social life, such as it is, conforms entirely to the cold-blooded model used by sociobiology and extrapolated to all life by Michael Ghiselin in the passage quoted above. They have very small brains (though large enough to outwit a fisherman) and a small repertoire of behaviour patterns controlled by a few and simple drives. I once caught a small perch using its own eyeball as bait. As a small boy I was fishing off a jetty, using worms for bait, and hooked one

---

10 The story is given in Hull, *Science as a Process*, citing Ghiselin, *The Economy of Nature* (1974 edn.), p. 247.

perch so small that the hook went into its eyeball, which came out when I unhooked it. Rather than kill the fish, I put it back in the water, in the hope that it would survive, and left the eyeball on the hook as a rather cold-blooded experiment. The first fish that took the bait was the very one I had just released. That time I killed it, and from then on I preferred to fish without bait at all. Yet even fish are capable of co-operative behaviour.

This comes in three sorts, corresponding to the three main mechanisms recognised by sociobiology. One is simply explained as an unintended consequence of numerous individual acts of self-preservation. Many species shoal, to avoid predators. George Williams, who first defined the analytical gene, showed that this can be explained by the instinct of each individual fish to seek shelter close to a neighbour, so the co-operative or altruistic quality of shoaling turns out to be an emergent property of individually selfish (or at least fearful) acts. The co-operative shoal arises from the selfishness of its individual parts. Because all would rather their neighbours, not themselves, were eaten and act to make this likely, almost all of them are less likely to be eaten than if they were not part of the shoal.

Some fish display elaborate patterns of care for their offspring. This is of course a special and limiting case of kin selection.

Reciprocal altruism is a rather different mechanism. Among the fish of the Great Barrier Reef there are some species which allow other, smaller fish to clean their teeth and gills of food fragments and parasites. The cleaner fish are tiny – bite-sized relative to the fish whose teeth they pick – yet they are hardly ever eaten.[11]

---

11 See Dawkins, *The Selfish Gene*, pp. 186–7.

Kin selection in the Hamiltonian sense cannot explain this, because the mechanism of kin selection depends on the two parties being part of the same breeding population. The answer that Trivers came up with was based on the fact that in the long run both species of fish do benefit from their co-operation. The payoff for the larger fish is in the future, but it is real.

'Reciprocal altruism' is really a model of delayed payoffs in a mutually beneficial trading system. It is just as mutually profitable, and just as little altruistic, as banking. Like any system of credit, it depends on trust, and is vulnerable to cheating. So it requires some way to divide the world into insiders and outsiders. Among fish, the mechanism for this division appears to be originally territorial. The cleaned species have their own sites in the coral to which the cleaners return. A simple rule of not eating small fish in one particular place, perhaps arising originally from satiety, would let the process get started. The cleaners now further distinguish themselves from edible rivals by special markings and 'dances'. Note that this does not rely on foresight or calculation on the part of the fish. On the contrary, it is the rigidity of their behaviour patterns and lack of imagination and foresight that makes the evolution of reciprocal altruism possible. The more flexible, imaginative, and far-sighted creatures involved become, the greater is their ability to cheat, and the stronger the defences against cheating must become. This fact later became important in making predictions about the origins and limits of human altruism.

Wilson emerges from his autobiography, *Naturalist*, as a transparently nice man, who had no idea how many people he was about to upset, and how deeply, when he published *Sociobiology*. Maynard Smith realised as soon as he saw a copy that there would be trouble, but this was because he had been a Communist Party member like his mentor J. B. S. Haldane. The two men did not finally leave the party until the invasion of Hungary in 1956, though they had taken little active part in party affairs after 1945.[12] It was then an item of Marxist dogma that human nature was overwhelmingly formed by culture, not by genetics. Wilson was not a genetic determinist: on the contrary, he believed that cultural factors probably do more to shape human possibilities than genetics do. In the jargon of those times, he thought Nurture more important than Nature. But he thought Nature mattered; and even this concession was anathema to Marxists. Their hostility came as a complete and terrible surprise to him. Two of the colleagues who rounded on his book had been friends in the Sixties: they had formed part of a group of five which retreated together into rural Vermont to plan the reformation of biology on mathematical grounds; they were then so close that they planned to write papers under a common pseudonym.[13]

Maynard Smith, with an eye for historical ironies, says that Wilson was partly a victim of McCarthyism: because communism had been driven so far underground in America during the Fifties and Sixties that most academics had no idea what it was actually like, or how Marxists thought, even though Richard Lewontin and Richard Levins, two of Wilson's friends and collaborators in Vermont, were themselves Marxists and became his most savage critics. Wilson and his supporters were later to see themselves as victims of McCarthyism in another sense: that they were honest scholars persecuted for political reasons.

'I had no interest in ideology', Wilson later wrote. 'My

---

12 Maynard Smith, interview with the author.
13 This collectivist scheme was soon abandoned.

purpose was to celebrate diversity and to demonstrate the intellectual power of evolutionary biology. Being an inveterate encyclopedist, I felt an additional obligation to include the human species. As I proceeded, I recognized an opportunity: the animal chapters would gain intellectual weight from their relevance to human behaviour. At some point I turned the relationship around; I came to believe that evolutionary biology should serve as the foundation of the social sciences.'[14]

In the meantime, his erstwhile friends Lewontin and Levins were moving in the other direction. In the throes of the Vietnam war, they came to believe that science was in fact serving political purposes. Both men resigned from the American Academy of Sciences in protest against the links between the government, the companies which financed much research and the war in Vietnam. They were members of a radical Leftist group called Science for the People which early engaged itself against what it regarded as science that served oppression. It was of course part of their faith that good science could not mandate injustice; bad science, they believed, might appear to do so and would gain much of its popularity from this fact. Almost any means were justified in this battle.

In 1975 the original reviews of *Sociobiology* were extremely favourable. A front-page article in the *New York Times* treated it as a news story: a new science would be born. The reaction from Science for the People was correspondingly savage. In a letter to the *New York Review of Books* the Science for the People Sociology Study Group accused the book of fascist tendencies. 'These recurrent determinist theories . . . consistently tend to provide a

---

14 *Naturalist*, p. 336.

genetic justification of the *Status Quo* and of existing privileges for certain groups according to class, race or sex. Historically, powerful countries or ruling groups within them have drawn support for the maintenance or extension of their power from those products of the scientific community. Such theories provided an important basis for the enactment of sterilization laws and restrictive immigration laws by the United States between 1910 and 1930 and also for the eugenics policies which led to the establishment of gas chambers in Nazi Germany.

'These theories operate as powerful forms of legitimation of past and present social institutions such as aggressive competition, domination of women by men, defense of national territory, and the appearance of a status and wealth hierarchy.'[15] And, they believed, *Sociobiology*, where it dealt with humans, was bad science too.

Wilson certainly saw his opponents as intellectual vigilantes, out to whip up a lynch mob. 'What I had said was defensible as science. The attack on it was political, not evidential. The Sociobiology Study Group had no interest in the subject beyond discrediting it.'[16]

The enmities made in that struggle persist to this day and so do some of the alliances. Wilson worked independently of the British sociobiologists, Hamilton, Maynard Smith, and Richard Dawkins, and there are disagreements within this group, but they are all broadly sympathetic to the idea that evolutionary biology can at last put the study of human nature on a scientific basis. They all see themselves – or at least their ideas – as persecuted. Most are passionately anti-religious, or at least passionately opposed to modern

---

15 *New York Review of Books*, 30 October 1975.
16 *Naturalist*, p. 339.

Protestantism, which, like its adherents, they take to be the only true religion. Their opponents are more ecumenically atheist. They do not even believe in science as an expression of religious yearning.

These two parties need names, and I propose to call them Gouldians and Dawkinsians. This won't please anyone involved. They will point out that the parties in question are vague and disorganised; that they don't have leaders and that if they did the candidates would be the men who got most respect as scientists in each party: Maynard Smith, perhaps, and Lewontin, not Dawkins and Gould. All this is true. But the fact remains that the parties do exist, and that Stephen Jay Gould and Richard Dawkins are not only their most visible proponents but also essential to defining them. Each man has in his rhetoric given enormous hostages to fortune. Both have written things which seem to their opponents to be unforgivable oversimplifications or flights of windy rhetoric.

To the extent that everyone interested in these questions is either a Gouldian or a Dawkinsian, the litmus test to decide which party they belong to is to ask them not whether it is Gould or Dawkins who most truly captures the scope and spirit of Darwinism but the opposite – which writer has done more damage to popular understanding of Darwinism. It would be difficult to find any working biologist who found this question unanswerable.

Other names for these parties have been proposed. It might seem simpler to call the Dawkinsians 'sociobiologists' but that would imply a continuity of doctrine which is not really there. Their testable scientific beliefs about human nature have changed and been considerably refined since Wilson's book came out.

To call the Dawkinsians 'Darwinian fundamentalists', as Gould does, is an inspired piece of polemical mud-slinging, but neither fair nor accurate. For one thing, the dismal view of human nature which the early sociobiologists promoted could stand quite independently of Darwin, and be reached by people who knew nothing of him, such as Machiavelli. For another, Gould claims Darwin himself as a sympathiser with his own catholic view of evolutionary processes.

On the other side, Dawkinsian philosophers like Helena Cronin and Daniel Dennett do tend to describe those who agree with them as 'Darwinian' (you can hear the capital letter when they speak) and only in passing to concede that their opponents are Darwinian too, at least in the sense of not being Creationist. Both sides, in fact, claim to be the true heirs of Darwin, and put up good arguments to this effect. But their quarrels range far more widely than mere historical legitimacy. They encompass not only arguments about scientific fact – these are in some ways the least important – but disagreements about the role and purpose of science, and personal animosities too. These elements mix unpredictably. There are friendships across parties and there have been quarrels within them. But, despite their fuzziness, the contending parties do clearly exist.

Like the original sociobiologists, their opponents form a well-defined group, held together by bonds of friendship and mutual esteem as much as by ideological agreement. The key opponents of adaptationism were Richard Lewontin, Stephen Jay Gould, and Steven Rose, disparate figures from differing areas of biology. Gould was a palaeontologist, Lewontin, a biologist, and Rose, an Englishman now professor of biology at the Open University, started off as a neuroscientist who was drawn into the field by the controversies over how much of IQ is inherited. It is relevant that all are Jewish and were more or less Marxist: being Jewish gave them a historical reason to be suspicious of anything reminiscent of a traditional eugenic way of thinking. Being Marxist gave them a strong bias against any theory which saw human biological nature as more important than human culture.

Stephen Jay Gould, one of the leaders of the opposition, was at least as ambitious as Wilson. Like Wilson, he has ended up working at the Museum of Comparative Zoology at Harvard. But he was in most other ways his opposite: a New York Jew, the urban child of Marxist parents, and always eager to sign up for the awkward squad, whereas Wilson reminisces fondly about his time as an Eagle Scout and education in a military academy. Wilson grew up a lover of live insects; Gould of extinct dinosaurs. Both men like to show off their erudition; as well as his technical work on land snails, and his general work on evolutionary theory, Gould had written on a huge range of subjects, from baseball to seventeenth-century Puritan theology. Yet the astonishing thing about Gould as a show-off is that he gets his facts right;[17] and he combines this accuracy with a voracious sympathy for his subjects. This wide-ranging mix of fluency and accuracy has given him a huge public. He has as an essayist a happy, Mozartian knack of making you think without realising you've done so. That is one reason for colleagues to loathe him.

Another is his controversial skill. His sympathies are extended to opponents only after their deaths. While they are alive, he can make them wish him dead, as so many of them appear to do. What especially maddens them is that he

---

17 Wilson sprinkles his more ambitious work with bum notes. For instance, he says in *Consilience* (p. 24) that England 'passed tumultuously from a feudal society to a nation-state' during the lifetime of Francis Bacon (1561–1626). It will come as news to historians that Elizabeth I inherited a feudal kingdom.

spends as much time writing about scientists as about science. As his friend Lewontin put it recently: 'Gould is primarily concerned with what the nature of organisms, living and dead, can reveal about the social construction of scientific knowledge. His repeated demonstrations that organisms can only be understood as historically contingent, underdetermined Rube Goldberg devices are meant to tell us more about the evolution of human knowledge than of human anatomy. From his early *Mismeasure of Man*, which examined how the political and social prejudices of prominent scientists have moulded what those scientists claimed to be the facts of human anatomy and intelligence, to his recent collection of essays, *Eight Little Piggies*, which despite its subtitle, *Reflections on Natural History*, is a set of reflections on the intellectual history of Natural History, Gould's deep preoccupation is with how knowledge, rather than the organism, is constructed.'[18]

His opponents put a similar point rather differently. 'Gould occupies a rather curious position, particularly on his side of the Atlantic. Because of the excellence of his essays, he has come to be seen by non-biologists as the preeminent evolutionary theorist. In contrast, the evolutionary biologists with whom I have discussed his work tend to see him as a man whose ideas are so confused as to be hardly worth bothering with, but as one who should not be publicly criticised because he is at least on our side against the creationists. All this would not matter, were it not that he is giving non-biologists a largely false picture of the state of evolutionary theory,' wrote John Maynard Smith[19] in a

---

18 *New York Review of Books*, 9 January 1998.
19 Review of *Darwin's Dangerous Idea*, by Daniel Dennett, *New York Review of Books*, 30 November 1995.

passage since gleefully requoted by endless Dawkinsians and Dawkins himself.

The general charge against Gould is that he has overstated the importance of his own theories. The philosopher and historian of science David Hull points out that there are two ways in which a scientist can try and spread a new idea: he can claim that it is an uncontroversial and natural development of what everyone already believes, or he can market it as a revolution, whose strength is derived from the fact that only a chosen vanguard understand it.[20] Both strategies have been adapted by both sides in these disputes, but Gould himself has tended to claim that his novel ideas are revolutionary, whereas Dawkins has preferred to argue that his are simply what everyone believed all along without noticing. Hull concluded his discussion with the delicate, dry observation that it was impossible to discern any correlation between the originality claimed for an idea and that which it might actually possess.

Other assessments of Gould's originality have been less polite. According to some of his enemies, he is meant to have supplanted orthodox Darwinism, as practised by working scientists, with a self-aggrandising construct of his own.[21] To some extent this is an inevitable consequence of writing about people still alive. As a journalist you can hope to make

---

20 *Science as a Process*, p. 484.

21 There, of course, is a symmetry with Dawkins here. Compare Lewontin's remark that 'Dawkins's vulgarizations of Darwinism speak of nothing in evolution but an inexorable ascendancy of genes that are selectively superior, while the entire body of technical advance in experimental and theoretical evolutionary genetics of the last fifty years has moved in the direction of emphasizing non-selective forces in evolution' (review of *The Demon-haunted World: Science as a Candle in the Dark*, by Carl Sagan, *New York Review of Books*, 9 January 1997).

people laugh at your descriptions of them, but you never hope that all your subjects will consider you just. Historians have their problems, but at least they do not usually have to consider the *amour propre* of their subjects.

The theory that has most upset people was his earliest, produced in conjunction with Niles Eldredge when both were palaeontologists working in New York, in 1972. Punctuated equilibrium claimed that there was a problem with the appearance of species in the fossil record: they persist in a largely stable form, for millions of years after their emergence. What is odd about this is that, if the Darwinian process were one of continuous friction-free adaptation, you would expect all species to be constantly evolving into their successors. This does not seem to happen. Instead, the fossil record shows clear breaks between species, which emerge suddenly and from nowhere in geological terms.

Of course, geological suddenness is perfectly compatible with gradual change across generations. The one thing this theory is not, and has never been claimed to be, is an attack on natural selection. On the contrary, one of the unstated premises of the theory is the efficiency of Darwinian selection as an agent of change: it is precisely because neo-Darwinism has found a process to develop whales from amoebas that we need an explanation for the persistence of amoebas, or of horseshoe crabs, which seem to have maintained their present form for around 200 million years while almost every other species around at the time of their arrival has gone extinct, along with most of the ones that flourished in the meantime. But the theory is and was meant as a challenge to the then reigning interpretation of Darwinism in which the persistence was an uninteresting problem.

Various mechanisms have since been proposed to account

for it. But the fact that there is something that needs explaining is now generally admitted. A measure of the theory's success is that its opponents now accept it fully and deny there was anything new or interesting about it. The Dawkinsians are confident that the persistence of species can be explained without in any way diminishing the primacy of gene-based explanations.

At the same time as he was active in the opposition to *Sociobiology*, Gould started hostilities with Richard Dawkins over the issue of gene selection. The analytical genes used by Dawkins, Hamilton and Maynard Smith all derive from the definition proposed by George Williams in 1966: a gene would be any length of DNA that is visible to a selection process. In this sense 'selfish gene' is partly a tautology, for Dawkins sometimes uses 'selfish' to mean 'visible to selection processes' too. The confusions and quarrels to which that gave rise are the subject of another chapter.

But it also seemed to follow from this definition that genes are the only thing which is selected. They are what natural selection, in the last analysis, is about. Indeed, the Dawkinsian definition of evolution is that it consists in changing frequencies of genes in the gene pool. Against this, Gould and others argued that it was meaningless to talk about natural selection working on genes, as against bodies, since genes are not and can never be directly selected.

It was bodies, whose characteristics are determined by a whole ensemble of genes, that natural selection discriminates between. Therefore it was inadequate to talk about genes being selected. That was not all that is going on.

Dawkins responded that he had never meant to deny this. He wanted only to point out that it is genes which are copied, not organisms. From the point of view of evolution, organisms do not exist: they are too short-lived, too unstable, and too unfaithfully copied. So only genes persist for long enough to be selected.

The easiest way to illustrate this dispute is by an analogy which Dawkins originally used in another context. Genomes are like recipes. Bodies are like cakes. The original, and important, point of this analogy was to argue against the idea that there were simple correspondences between genes and bodies. If genes were like blueprints for buildings, as opposed to recipes, you could add something to the blueprint and know what effect it would have on the building. Conversely, you can look at a building and reconstruct its blueprint. This makes reverse engineering possible and would, if biology were like that, make Lamarckianism possible in principle. But biology is not like that. You cannot reconstruct a genotype from a phenotype because the only way to find out what phenotype you get from a genotype is to grow it.

You cannot read the cake directly off the recipe, and if you change the ingredients or the cooking methods, the cake will change in unpredictable ways. It is impossible to point to part of a finished cake and claim that it corresponds to a particular ingredient or cooking process. All this corresponds to the varied and complicated effects that genes have when constructing bodies.

Yet if we look at the history of cooking, what has survived are not cakes, but recipes. So the Dawkinsians argue that only recipes have been selected. Cakes are merely eaten. Against this, the Gouldians would reply that there is no 'merely' involved. No one ever ate a recipe: selection acts on cakes, or bodies, and not on genes, or recipes.

Unusually enough, this dispute has now been resolved to the satisfaction of both sides. The key to it is realising that 'selection' can refer to both parts of what is a two-stage process. For natural selection to occur there must be competition among the things being selected among; and this involves both copying and winnowing. The winnowing determines what is copied. The copying determines what will be winnowed. But what is copied and what is winnowed are not the same. Genes (or recipes) are copied. Bodies (or cakes) are winnowed. And both processes are necessary for evolution.

Indeed, both sides will now tell you that this is what they meant all along. 'I can't imagine what it would mean to say that natural selection acted directly on genes,' says Helena Cronin, echoing Dawkins.[22]

---

22 It is actually possible to imagine one meaning of this phrase. Since genes themselves have phenotypes, consisting as they do of lengths of chromosome acting together to produce an effect, or several, in the body of an organism, it is possible to imagine that new genes could arise by the splitting into two of such a length of DNA, so that each part affected only one of the characteristics which are both affected by the present gene. If this allowed for more efficient selection of the resultant animal, I don't see why you couldn't speak of natural selection acting directly on genes.

4

MARXISTS AT THE MUSEUM

THE BITTEREST RIFT came between Wilson and his friend Richard Lewontin. This was doubly painful, since Wilson had urged that Harvard hire Lewontin, and assured his colleagues there that Lewontin's political activism would cause the university no trouble. Though he was a committed opponent of the Vietnam war, and was to become a Marxist, he was so brilliant that Wilson took for granted that his commitment to science would outweigh his political interests.

Lewontin as a young man had been the first person to suggest the application of game theory to evolutionary problems, in 1961:[1] the very avenue that Price, Maynard Smith and other Dawkinsians were later to explore with such success. He had also discovered the technique which enables scientists to measure how different the DNA of one organism is from another. This is a crude measure compared to the hopes of mapping whole genomes, which would eventually allow us to compare the DNA of different organisms just as my word-processor can compare two documents and produce an itemised list of all the differences between them.

---

1 David Hull, *Science as a Process*, p. 210.

But Lewontin's work points up one difficulty with this dream. The first thing these techniques of DNA analysis were used to discover was how much variation exists within a population of wild fruit flies, and the answer was 'far more than anyone had supposed'. This has been repeated across lots of organisms and turns out to be true for almost all of them. There is a great deal of genetic difference within species.

Much of it is not obvious. The genetic variations within human species do not correspond at all well to racial groups, so far as we can currently measure them. There is far more variation within races, on average, than there is between them. As Lewontin puts it: 'If humans are anything like experimental animals, about one in every 500 nucleotides will differ in DNA taken from any two individuals chosen at random. Since there are roughly 3 billion nucleotides in human genes, any two human beings will differ on the average in about 600,000 nucleotides. And an average gene that is, say, 3,000 nucleotides long will differ between any two normal individuals by about 20 nucleotides. Whose genome, then, is going to provide the sequence for the catalogue for the normal person?

'Moreover, every normal person carries a large number of defective genes in single doses inherited from one parent that are covered up by a normal copy that they received from their other parent. So any piece of DNA that is sequenced will have a certain number of unknown defective genes entered into the catalogue. When the DNA from a person with a disease is compared to the DNA from the standard normal sequence, it would be impossible to decide which if any of the multiple differences between the two DNAs is responsible for the disease. It would be necessary to look at a large population of normal and diseased people to see if one could find some common difference between them, but even this may not happen if the disease in question has a multiple genetic cause so that different people have the same disease for different reasons, even if all those reasons are a consequence of genetic changes.'[2]

This argument against the Human Genome Project was made much later than Lewontin's campaign against sociobiology but it shows a line of argument which has been consistent throughout his agitations, whether against IQ testing, sociobiology, or the Human Genome Project, and this is a distrust of the notion that there could ever be a perfect type of human. Populations vary all the time, and there is no perfection to be found among them.

In one form this is not a controversial doctrine. Without constant variation there would be nothing for selection to act on, so the rejection of perfection is part of Darwin's rejection of the fixity of species. But for Lewontin and his allies there was a deeper lesson to be learnt, and this was that all attempts to talk in terms of human nature are sinister as well as mistaken: they will justify injustice.

One has to be a little careful here. The spectacle of Marxists accusing anyone of ideas that can lead to atrocity can seem grotesque (especially in the light of Pol Pot's funeral pyre which illuminates the front page of the newspaper as I write this). Their opponents have made much of these grotesqueries. Richard Dawkins, reviewing *Not in Our Genes*, an attack on sociobiology by Lewontin, Rose, and the psychologist Leon J. Kamin, described it as 'a sort of scientific Dave Spart trying to get into Pseud's Corner'.[3]

---

2 Richard Lewontin, *The Doctrine of DNA*, p. 50.
3 *New Scientist*, 24 January 1985.

Yet Rose, Lewontin, and Gould, however clumsily they may on occasion express themselves, are surely right to ask about the social consequences of popular science, and to see science as a human activity taking place within existing societies and partly conditioned by them. Scientists are not priests, mediating selflessly between Nature and man. Considerations of funding, if nothing else, must ensure that scientists pay attention to problems the world thinks urgent as well as to those they themselves find interesting. As Lewontin tirelessly points out, many scientists have a direct financial interest in the spread of genetic explanations, for they own shares in companies which hope to exploit their research in the field.

The ways in which scientific discoveries, when they make their way in the world, turn out to have social consequences is nicely illustrated by the research that has led to very high-yielding strains of hybrid corn. Quite apart from its ecological consequences, hybrid corn has one important disadvantage from the farmer's point of view. It does not breed true. If you plant normal corn and it is successful, you can keep some back for seed. But with hybrid corn, you must return to the seed company and buy another batch of seed every year. It is, to use a computer analogy, copy-protected. It might have been possible to develop true-breeding corn with the desired properties; but this would have made far less money for the seedsmen who could have sold their product only once, instead of year after year. To Lewontin this fact is shocking. It is an example of science working to impoverish those farmers who cannot afford the hybrid corn, though it is of course sold to the public as an example of science working for the public good.

This kind of thing is especially painful to anyone raised in the tradition of the enlightened Left which holds that science is a moral force, whose practice and fruits must make the world better. If mere plant biology can turn out to conceal such capitalist iniquities, how much more dangerous might not human biology become? In the climate of the Seventies, one of the centrally shocking assertions of early human sociobiology was that human nature precludes equality. Understood as a political slogan, this meant, and has continued to mean, that there is no real point in doing very much for the poor and miserable.

The strong part of the Marxist case against sociobiology was not that there is no such thing as human nature, but that our understandings of it must be cultural, partial and subject to distortion: that 'Nature' as much as 'nurture' is a cultural construct. This is easier to see now, when both terms have fallen out of fashion and seem to be curious archaisms rather than eternal verities. It is also easier to see that the sorts of equality which human nature is thought to preclude will vary from time to time and from society to society: in any given context they will usually be those which would interfere most with the interests of the powerful.

The early campaign against sociobiology was largely successful by the early Eighties. The English philosopher Philip Kitcher's study of the early sociobiological claims, *Vaulting Ambition*, first published in 1985, was a scrupulously fair and crushing study that ground into the dust the claims of human sociobiologists actually to have established what they claimed to, though Kitcher concluded that a Darwinian analysis of human nature was an inevitable and indeed a desirable project: it just hadn't been done well enough. Other reasons for the discredit were disgraceful. The supporters of Science for the People were quite happy to intimidate their opponents. In the worst incident, a group of black Maoist student protesters mounted the platform at a scientific meeting where Gould and Wilson were debating and drenched Wilson (who had a broken leg at the time) with water. Wilson told the audience he felt as if he had been speared by an aborigine. They then chanted, 'E. O. Wilson, you can't hide. We charge you with genocide!' for a while.[4] This probably represented the nadir of the Marxist case.

This, though, was also the period when the sociobiological case was at its weakest and most naïve. The problem was that sociobiology explained too much and predicted too little.[5] It is possible to find adaptive explanations for almost any human trait: even our preferences in estate agents can be reduced to a toolkit of aptitudes for surviving on the savannah: a fine example of this tradition is Steven Pinker's book *How the Mind Works*, published in 1997. Pinker is a linguist at MIT, which may explain why he sees so few difficulties in applying adaptationist explanations to all biological and social problems: in one place he solemnly explains that the reason why millionaires like penthouses with expansive views over the countryside is that such places would have appealed to our ancestors when they were cave-hunting.

The objection to this stuff is not that it isn't true: it may be. But so might the exactly opposite proposition be: Bill Gates builds a low house, clinging to the ground; is this because his ancestors felt more secure concealed in long grass? Human beings are undoubtedly better adapted to give birth in modern maternity hospitals than in caves, in the sense that far more children born in such circumstances survive. Does that mean we evolved in maternity hospitals?

---

4 According to Val Dusek, a Gouldian who was present at the attack.
5 For a detailed account, see Kitcher's *Vaulting Ambition*. But you will have to get it from a library; unlike most of the works mentioned, it is thoroughly out of print.

Pinker's book, though published in 1997, is very much a throwback to the earlier style of pop sociobiology. The disputes over this kind of adaptive explanation are deeper and older. Gould and Lewontin, in 1979, published a paper attacking the whole concept of adaptation. 'The Spandrels of San Marco' took its title from some Venetian frescos: a spandrel is a small area 'left over' when a dome is raised on two intersecting arches. The spandrel simply appears, by geometric necessity, as a by-product of that sort of arch.[6] The painter of the ceiling of San Marco found a way to incorporate these areas into his grander design and the result is wonderful. It looks as if that is what the spandrels were made for. But of course this is misleading: their purpose is not the same as their cause.

Gould and Lewontin argued that animals, as much as architecture, might display 'spandrels': features of form or behaviour which had no adaptive function, but were a necessary by-product of something else that had. They mocked the ambitions of sociobiologists to find adaptive explanations of every interesting fact about human beings. For example, our capacity for geometry is an important explanation for the spread and success of the human species. It is genetically specified, in as much as it appears in any normally developing human brain. But it was certainly not selected for when our ancestors were evolving our characteristic normality in Africa. It is a spandrel, but one which has played an important role in the success of our species.

The fact of spandrels is not disputed: neither is the fact of

---

6 Daniel Dennett, incidentally, devotes several pages of *Darwin's Dangerous Idea* to the task of proving that the feature Gould calls a 'spandrel' is actually known to the architects as something else.

'exaptations', another Gould coinage, which describes organs which are selected for one use, but which acquire a new one (and so a new kind of selection pressure) as a result of a change in an organism's surroundings or behaviour. The classic example is the evolution of feathers, which started off as cooling devices on small dinosaurs and ended up as flying devices on birds. What is disputed is their importance and interest.

The beauty and power of natural selection as an explanation of complexity are that it enables us to deduce the causes of things from their function; but this only works when the function is clearly defined. In some cases, the function of an organ is obvious; and when this is true, natural selection can accomplish prodigies of design. A spider's web and a human eye are extraordinarily successful and intricate adaptations to fairly obvious problems. In other cases, adaptations can be understood as serving functions which are not at all obvious. This second category includes most of the discoveries of Evolutionary Psychology, a discipline that descends from sociobiology (it is discussed in Chapter Seven).

But three areas of adaptation remain controversial. The first is what sorts of complexity it can explain. The second is that adaptations can often only be spotted in hindsight. The third, which is related, is to do with the balance between adaptive processes and initial conditions. How far can adaptation get you from where you start?

The first problem is part of the subject matter of Dawkins's *The Extended Phenotype*, which offers one clear solution that Gouldians reject. To see the difficulty, consider the difference between an ant's eye and an ants' nest. Both may be considered as the product of ant genes. This is what Dawkins meant by his title. Some genes, through a long cascade of chemical causes, will make ant tissues behave in such a way that they turn into eyes. Others will cause ant brains to grow in such a way that the resulting ant uses its eyes to help it make nests. Changes in specific functional genes will cause the eye or brain to grow differently, and thus cause changes in behaviour patterns. So these can be considered analytically as genes 'for' particular behaviours, which will have differing effects on the survival of the ants and so of their genes. Dawkins argued that it makes no difference whether the crucial phenotypic consequences of a gene – the ones that have an effect on fitness – take place inside or outside the ant. The ants' nest is as much an effect of their genes as their eyes are. Or, to extend the phenotype still further, certain tobacco genes are selected not because of their effect on tobacco plants so much as for their effect on human tissues. In any domesticated plant, the crucial phenotypic effects, which determine whether a particular gene will be selected, take place inside human bodies and brains. The route by which increasing nicotine yields come to be adaptive for tobacco plants runs through human lungs.

It is easy enough to see the purpose of an ant's eye and conclude that it is an adaptation to the problem of seeing. In a similar way, you can look at a tobacco allele that produces more nicotine than its rival and conclude that it is an adaptation to the problems of getting humans to cultivate the plant. But what is the purpose of an ants' nest or of a whole tobacco plant? Is it possible to answer the question of what it is designed to do except in the vaguest terms?

The Dawkinsian answer would be that the nest is designed to transmit ant genes; and that so, ultimately, is the ant's eye. Tobacco plant genes are propagated by the addictive effects of tobacco on humans, so the purpose of these effects must be to propagate tobacco genes. This is an answer which appeals to the same mechanism as the argument from function of parts of an organism, yet it seems to the Gouldians to extend it illegitimately. They would say that adaptation requires constraints. It is always an adaptation to a particular problem; and to stretch the concept to cover so general a problem as 'the survival of ant genes' makes it too thin to be any use. As the philosopher Jerry Fodor (in this context a Gouldian) put it: 'There's a lot of "because" out there, but there isn't any "for" . . . it's very difficult to get this right because our penchant for explaining things on the model of agents, with their beliefs, goals, and desires – is inveterate and probably itself innate. We are forever wanting to know what things are for and we don't like having to take Nothing for an answer.'[7]

This is a difficult objection for Dawkinsians to grasp. Their difficulty is exemplified by the philosopher Daniel Dennett, whose book *Darwin's Dangerous Idea* is as clear an expression as you could hope to find of the Dawkinsian programme (and of unremitting personal hostility to Gould). He believes his opponents are denying the power of natural selection to produce really complicated things. The central metaphor of his book is a contrast between 'cranes' and 'sky-hooks': skyhooks are naughty and magical, invoking unknown properties, while cranes are good, algorithmic, and material. Cranes are scientific, skyhooks religious. Cranes explain problems; skyhooks proclaim mysteries. It makes for a lot of good knockabout fun but it misses the main point. Gouldians don't doubt the role of natural selection in solving problems: they doubt its role in setting them. Darwinian design can produce perfectly adapted structures of incredible complexity; what it cannot do is

7 Review of *Climbing Mount Improbable*, by Richard Dawkins, *London Review of Books*, 19 April 1996.

predict what problems will need to be solved.

Besides, an organism is trying to solve many different problems simultaneously, in that it is 'designed' to do many different things, and these may conflict with each other. It is not controversial among biologists that the solutions often involve compromises and trade-offs. Gould and Dawkins would both agree with Ernst Mayr, a grand old man of the previous generation of biologists, who wrote: 'There is a cost to every evolutionary advance (such as running faster, having more offspring, utilising a new source of food) and selection determines whether or not the added advantage is worth the cost.'[8]

But Mayr goes on to argue, in a more Gouldian way, that 'The result is that the phenotype is often a patchwork of features that were specifically selected for a particular function (or as the answer to a particular selection pressure) and others that are the by-product of the genotype as a whole and are simply tolerated by selection. From Darwin's time on, naturalists have asked themselves into which of the two categories they should class differences among species. For instance, is the difference in the striping of Burchell's and Grevy's zebra a result of different selection pressures in the different parts of Africa where these species originated, or, as is more likely, was there simply a selection for striping to which the genotypes of the two species responded differently?

'As long as certain geneticists believed in an independent fitness of every gene, each having one optimal fitness value, one could believe that every aspect of the phenotype was the appropriate response to ad hoc selection. But the fact that the individual as a whole is the target of selection, and,

---

8 Ernst Mayr, *The Growth of Biological Thought*, p. 590.

furthermore, that many (if not all) genes are interacting with each other, sets severe limits for the response of the phenotype to selection. That is why man still has an appendix, a vulnerable sacro-iliac joint, and poorly built sinuses.'[9]

This is perhaps only a difference of emphasis from the adaptationists. But it has a curious and noteworthy analogy in disputes among economists. Natural selection is a mechanism that produces the *best* answers to questions that have no *right* answers. So, in classical economics, is a market. Just as economists expect the natural condition of a market is to clear, so strong adaptationists expect that the natural end of a selective process is perfect adaptation. Both classical economists and adaptationists admit the existence of friction in the real world; but they don't think it really matters. Their opponents, in both cases, disagree.

And though there is no necessary correlation between political views and a position in evolutionary biology, there is an obvious overlap of meaning in such terms as 'selfish'. The language of biology has been used ever since Darwin to defend or elaborate economic theories. It is certainly the case that the rhetoric of 'selfishness' as a law that applied all across the natural world was used to justify and reinforce superficially similar economic theories in the Thatcher/Reagan years. This was not the intention of any of the founders of selfish gene theory.

The business of adaptation is still further complicated, as both Gould and Lewontin point out, because the relationship between an organism and its environment is not a passive one, in which the environment poses problems which the organism then solves, or fails to. The organism

9 Ibid.

helps to make its own environment. It changes the world that surrounds it, and to some extent it chooses the surroundings it will change. The enormous stress on the importance of genes, as opposed to bodies, means that Dawkinsians or strong adaptationists often talk as if the world of actual living organisms were like a contest between computer programs with the genes as programmers.

Such competitions do exist in real computers and have played an important part in the development of socio-biological theory. A lot of the models of reciprocal altruism were developed by simply setting different programs to compete against each other inside a machine and seeing which won. And this is clearly the best way to abstract away to the strategies that an organism might be using and to study them. If nothing else, it tells you what to look for in the real world. But an organism is more than the sum of its strategies.

This is not just a metaphysical point to the Gouldians. They would say that not only an organism's being but also its behaviour is more than the sum of its strategies: at least, that simple strategies may interact in complex ways to produce unpredictably complex ones and that this matters fundamentally. It's a belief that has obvious analogies with Marxism, since it might be put as 'quantity alters quality'. This heritage doesn't necessarily make it untrue. In fact Dawkinsians recognise emergent qualities as much as anyone else.[10] It's just that they don't believe they are interesting. This seems to Gouldians a piece of philosophical confusion. The whole point of emergent properties is that they cannot be reduced to their constituent parts. They represent a

---

10 Emergent qualities are those which appear when you add together things which individuals do not have. The classic example is the wetness of water: nothing about an individual molecule of H_2O is wet.

threshold over which a reduction cannot step.

If by 'evolution' is meant the whole history of life on earth, then, to the Gouldian mind, an over-arching theory would need to explain what sort of problems organisms have had to solve as well as how they solved them. It would deal with ecology and the interactions between species as well as the adaptations within species. They want explanations for undesigned complexity, and for the ecological aspects of biology. Dawkinsians don't see the need for over-arching theories or laws of historical development. Maynard Smith, as an ex-Marxist and so a former believer in huge laws, is particularly scathing. He dismisses complexity theory, a currently fashionable way to explain how order, or at least organisation, can arise spontaneously from chaos, as 'Absolute fucking crap. But crap with good PR.'[11]

He would, I think, say that there are certain important things for which no theory is possible. They just happen. This is an attitude with which Gouldians can live. What drives them to a frenzy is the suggestion that algorithmic Darwinism – Dennett's mechanism of cranes – is itself the large-scale law that explains development.

The second problem with adaptation is that it is always a retrospective explanation. Gould and Lewontin have often used a form of intellectual ju-jitsu which turns the strength of adaptationist argument against itself. They point out that the weakness of adaptationist argument is that it explains too much. What is needed is not a mechanism to produce answers, for adaptationist explanations can answer anything, but a mechanism to specify the questions more rigorously.

Of course, in practice, the two processes are quite closely coupled. The answer to a question such as 'How important

---

11 Personal communication, walking back from the pub.

is adaptation?' is as much a matter of temperament and philosophical interest as it is of fact. As a rule,[12] Dawkinsians are interested in rules, Gouldians in exceptions. Dawkinsians will stress the power and reliability of natural selection, and its ability to produce adaptations to almost anything: Gouldians will reply that there are large numbers of starting points eliminated by chance or mass extinction, and that in consequence there is much that natural selection will never be able to accomplish.

'I do not deny that natural selection has helped us to explain phenomena at scales very distant from individual organisms, from the behaviour of an ant colony to the survival of a redwood forest', Gould wrote. 'But selection cannot suffice as a full explanation for many aspects of evolution; for other types and styles of causes become relevant, or even prevalent, in domains both far above and far below the traditional Darwinian locus of the organism. Those other causes are not, as the ultras often claim, the product of thinly veiled attempts to smuggle purpose back into biology. These additional principles are as directionless, non-teleological and materialistic as natural selection itself – but they operate differently from Darwin's central mechanism. In other words, I agree with Darwin that natural selection is "not the exclusive means of modification".'[13]

Precisely because this dispute is so much a matter of style and world view, it is peculiarly hard to resolve. There really are very few disputes between the two sides about scientifically establishable facts. The characteristic reaction of one side to some assertion by the other is not so much 'That can't be true' as 'Of course it's true. So what?' Again and

---

12 To which there are exceptions.
13 'Darwinian Fundamentalism', p. 34.

again, when talking to the people involved, I have been struck by how little they understand of their opponents' motivations. They just can't see why certain facts or arguments matter to the other side.

Broad factual agreement does not make these disputes trivial. In part, they are about what sort of research makes interesting science; and so what people should be paid to do. They affect the livelihood and the reputation of the protagonists in the deepest possible sense. Academic disputes are savage not because so little is at stake, but because so much is: they are about honour as much as about truth.[14]

---

14 This is itself a sort of sociobiological explanation, if 'honour' means status among men of fighting age. In a species where mating success among males is determined by their status, Richard Lovelace was not romantic but completely down-to-earth when, in his poem 'To Lucasta, Going to the Wars', he wrote: 'I could not love thee, Dear, so much,/Loved I not honour more.' If he had had no honour, Lucasta would not have cared at all whether he loved her.

5

SOME TYPES OF SELFISHNESS

IT IS AN extraordinary comment on the state of the social sciences in the 1960s that the rehabilitation of human nature should have been a task originally undertaken by entomologists. Wilson and Hamilton were both men whose fieldwork was done with insects, and whose fascination with ants and minute wasps shines through their reminiscences. But there were philosophers interested in the matter, too; and one of the most formidable was an Englishwoman named Mary Midgley. She taught at Newcastle with her husband Geoffrey, for nearly thirty years, but retained the unforgiving self-confidence of an Oxford don throughout this period. I think of her picking her way through the confusions of the world in her large, sensible shoes with a lorgnette in one hand and a flick knife in the other. Her capacity for scrupulous examination of a question is equalled only by her gift for an eviscerating phrase.

In the late Sixties, she found herself deeply frustrated by the orthodoxy of the Left that there is no such thing as human nature: that in essence we are entirely formed by our environment. 'Educated opinion on this topic seemed split into two impossible extreme positions. And of the two I was *more* shocked (as one is) by the gratuitous folly of my own tribe, the humanists and social scientists, in swallowing Skinnerian blank paper theory [the idea that human beings were born with almost infinitely malleable nature and could be moulded by their upbringings into any shape at all] . . . It seemed to me madness to throw away all chance of having anything sensible to say about human nature just because Desmond Morris and Robert Ardrey were saying mistaken things about it.'[1]

So she started to teach a course, first to adults, and then to undergraduates in the course of a short stay at Cornell, in which these questions were addressed. How can we be free, reasoning beasts? It must be possible to be such things, since we are. But it is not clear how we manage the trick. Her lectures at Cornell turned into a book, *Beast and Man*, which was nearly ready when *Sociobiology* was published. Her publishers, combining, as publishers do, rationality and beastliness in defence of their own interests, asked her to take account of the latter, and she ended up rewriting almost the whole of *Beast and Man*.

In one sense Midgley's programme was profoundly opposed to the ambitions of sociobiology. Wilson had hoped to reduce all subjects to biology, or at least to rebuild them anew on a biological base: Midgley was hostile both in principle and in practice to the attempt. Philosophy informed by biology was not a subdivision of biology, in her view, but a better sort of philosophy, an enterprise in which biological competence was no guarantee of success. This did not mean she thought it was a matter that should concern only philosophers. Moral philosophy appeared to her something like prose: we all produce it all the time, whether or not we are paid to do so. It is necessary for all of us to improve it.

---

1 Personal communication.

But she also believed that human nature existed, and that it was overwhelmingly important to get as accurate an idea of it as possible. In this she was squarely on the side of the sociobiologists, and opposed to the shenanigans of Science for the People on strategic as well as tactical grounds: 'It seemed to me *far* madder, far less fertile, to try to do without a notion of human nature altogether (as the social scientists wanted to do) than to start with a crude notion of Human Nature which might be refined later.'[2]

The belief that there is such a thing as human nature and that we can learn as much about it from novelists, historians, and philosophers as we can from scientists may seem unsurprising to people who read books (and even to people who don't) but it entails a surprising number of academic heresies. Midgley spent most of the Seventies fending off attacks from philosophers who thought her too scientific and scientists who thought she was making too much of philosophy and no doubt from other people who thought she wrote too well. One of the pleasures of researching this story is the amount of clear and vigorous writing the subject provokes. The combatants in the Darwin wars know what they want to say and that it is urgent. They write from conviction, not for hire; this fact alone would make their books stand out from almost everything else on sale. But no one brings more vividness to their clarity than Midgley. It is a pity, then, that her 'Gene Juggling', her long discussion of the first edition of *The Selfish Gene*, published in *Philosophy* in 1979, used the flick knife and the stout boots rather more than the lorgnette. She had not meant it as a book review: what worried her was that the sloppy philosophising in the book was corrupting the judgement of professional

---

2 Personal communication.

philosophers. But Dawkins understood it as a review of his efforts, and so did others.

The last footnote gives a flavour of the thing: 'Up till now, I have not attended to Dawkins, thinking it unnecessary to break a butterfly upon a wheel. But Mr Mackie's article is not the only indication I have lately met of serious attention paid to his fantasies.'[3] What went before this footnote had not been noticeably kinder. 'There is nothing empirical about Dawkins. Critics have repeatedly pointed out that his notions of genetics are unworkable. His central point is that the emotional nature of man is exclusively self-interested, and he argues this by claiming that all emotional nature is so. Since the emotional nature of animals is clearly not exclusively self-interested, nor based on any long-term calculation at all, he resorts to arguing from speculations about the emotional nature of genes, which he treats as the source and archetype of all emotional nature.'[4]

This gets selfish gene theory, as a piece of biology, about as wrong as it can possibly be got. What is more, she persistently failed to understand the concept of the analytic gene that he was using. 'Dawkins's crude, cheap, blurred genetics is not just an expository device. It is the kingpin of his crude, cheap, blurred psychology . . . Dawkins is no geneticist and . . . all the genetics which he or anyone knows is solidly opposed to his notion of genes as independent units, only contingently connected, and locked in constant internecine competition, a war of all against all. (In spite of some words in the last quotation, he cannot really mean that it is just war between each gene and its own alleles; this would allow co-operation over the rest of the field and

---

3 'Gene Juggling'.
4 Ibid.

destroy his case entirely.)'[5]

Whether or not her remarks were unforgivable, they certainly remain unforgiven. As late as 1992, Dawkins withdrew from a conference to which he had been invited, when he heard that Midgley would also be present. 'I wouldn't want to see her over breakfast,' he told the organiser.[6]

And she did get his biology quite wrong. In this, she may have had professional help: her paper credits a biologist colleague at Newcastle University with technical assistance, and the signs are that he utterly failed to understand Dawkins's use of the analytical as opposed to the functional gene idea. There was a page and a half of disquisition on just how many genes might be needed to control a particular behaviour pattern in bees. Dawkins, when he came to reply, had no difficulty in showing that this was confused and ignorant.

As we have seen, Dawkins did explain that 'selfishness' among genes was entirely compatible with mutual co-operation, and success often consisted in being more co-operative than rivals. This is not as ridiculous as it may sound: if one takes a situation in which both human selfishness and self-interest are possible – say the competition between two politicians – pure self-interest may lead to each behaving unselfishly, perhaps by building as large a coalition as possible, and trying to outdo his rivals in co-operative behaviour.[7]

5 Ibid.
6 John Cornwell, personal communication.
7 This self-interest may sometimes be combined with selfishness in a moral sense, though it may not: politicians are to varying degrees selfish in their pursuit of power. At least, they are on any interesting analysis of their character. Another reason for being careful about using the 'S' word.

Selfish gene theory can be used to show how genuine altruism can arise from an interplay of forces (or genes) which are incapable of it, or of any other feelings. In other contexts, and when it is put forward by other writers, Midgley understands this very well. But she read Dawkins as putting forward a kind of grand unifying theory, which would subsume all life forms from the bacterium to the biologist into the same kind of explanation. That may have been his ambition: but, if it was, the unifying principle he was looking for was genes, or things that worked like genes in as much as they were exposed to some kind of selective process. She read him as claiming it was selfishness, in a fairly ordinary sense, instead. 'He contends that the appearance of "a limited form of altruism at the level of individual animals", including ourselves, is only a deceptive phantom. The underlying reality, as he often says, is not any other individual motivation either, but the selfishness of the genes. Yet he just as often talks as if this established that the individual motivation were different from what it appears to be – as here, "we are born selfish". His thought seems to be that individual motivation is only an expression of some profounder, more metaphysical motivation, which he attributes to genes, and is bound therefore to represent it.'[8]

She quoted from *The Selfish Gene*: 'The argument of this book is that we, and all other animals, are machines created by our genes. Like successful Chicago gangsters, our genes have survived, in some cases for millions of years, in a highly competitive world. This entitles us to expect certain qualities of our genes. I shall argue that a predominant quality to be expected in our genes is ruthless selfishness.'[9]

---

8 'Gene Juggling'.
9 Ibid.

This really shocked her: 'Telling people that they are *essentially* Chicago gangsters is not just false and confused, but monstrously irresponsible. It can only mean that their feeble efforts to behave more decently are futile, that their conduct will amount to the same whatever they do, that their own and other people's apparently more decent feelings are false and hypocritical.

'Dawkins, however, claims innocence of all this. He says he is merely issuing a warning that we had better *resist* our genes and "upset their designs".

'Be warned that if you wish, as I do, to build a society in which individuals co-operate generously and unselfishly towards a common good, you can expect little help from our biological nature . . . let us understand what our own selfish genes are up to, because we may then at least have the chance to upset their designs.

'He does not explain who the "we" are that have somehow so far escaped being pre-formed by these all-powerful forces as to be able to turn against them; he does not even raise the question how we are supposed to conceive the idea of "building a society in which individuals co-operate generously and unselfishly towards a common good" if there were no kindly and generous feelings in our emotional make-up.'[10]

And it's true that there is no logical link between the picture of human nature and conduct suggested by the cloudy rhetoric of *The Selfish Gene* and the detailed and worked-out theories of genetics which it is the purpose of the book to expound. If you take all references to the 'selfishness' of genes out of the discussion of genetics, they lose nothing of their sense. If you take them out of the

10 Ibid.

references to human nature, these collapse in a heap. Yet Dawkins really did not set out to write about human motivation at all, and was astonished to be told that he had done so. He was still more astonished when Midgley entirely missed his detailed genetic reasoning.

In fact he was so hurt by her attack on him for egoism that he was for many years unable to bring himself to believe that she had actually read his book. His counterblast to her work, published in *Philosophy* two years later, opened on a note of hurt astonishment: 'I have been taken aback by the inexplicable hostility of Mary Midgley's assault. Some colleagues have advised me that such transparent spite is best ignored, but others warn that the venomous tone of her article may conceal the errors in its content. Indeed, we are in danger of assuming that nobody would dare to be so rude without taking the elementary precaution of being right.'[11]

He saw no signs of such caution in her work.

'Midgley raises the art of misunderstanding to dizzy heights. . . . When biologists talk about "selfishness" or "altruism" we are emphatically not talking about emotional nature, whether of human beings, other animals, or genes. We do not even mean the words in a *metaphorical* sense. We *define* altruism and selfishness in purely behaviouristic ways . . . philosophers may object that this kind of definition loses most of the spirit of what is ordinarily meant by altruism, but philosophers, of all people, know that words may be redefined in special ways for technical purposes.'[12]

Actually, I think Dawkins here underestimates his own originality. For a behaviouristic explanation of altruism is not the only, and not even the most important, sense in

---

11 Dawkins 'In Defence of Selfish Genes', p. 556.
12 Ibid.

which 'selfishness' is a central concept in his book. He also uses it as a universal term, to mean 'having a distinct identity on which selective processes can act'. To be selfish in this sense implies nothing whatever about psychology, motivation, or even behaviour. It simply means to be visible to – that is, a distinct subject of – Darwinian selection. This is an extremely important quality, and Dawkins's originality consisted in being the first person to stress its importance in all sorts of contexts. If he'd thought of an original name for it as well, he might have saved a lot of confusion, not all of it other people's.

'No reasonable philosopher would say, "I don't like your definition, therefore I shall interpret your statement as though you were using *my* definition; by my definition your concept of the selfish gene is nonsense, therefore it *is* nonsense." This is in effect what Midgley has done. "Genes cannot be selfish or unselfish, any more than atoms can be jealous, elephants abstract, or biscuits teleological." Why didn't she add to this witty little list, for the benefit of quantum physicists, that fundamental particles cannot have charm?'[13]

This may have been meant as a rhetorical question, but it drew a reply: 'Physicists can only use these terms because their new use is so far removed from their old one that there can be no possibility of interpreting their sentences in the old sense. So far from this being the case with selfishness, many if not most of the remarks made about it in the new sense admit of an interpretation in the old sense which sounds, not only intelligible, but attractively familiar. They read as ordinary statements and developments of psychological egoism. I am entirely prepared to believe that these interpretations come as a complete surprise to Dawkins in his

---

13 Ibid.

capacity as Dr Jekyll, the honourable and single-minded expounder of biological truths. Jekyll writes about half the book, and I ought to have paid tribute to him before, for doing it so well. Instead, perversely enough, I not only took him for granted but thought that his presence actually made things worse. How can a writer who can do this work so admirably then go on to spoil it with irrelevant rhetoric? And how is it possible for readers to feel that, with those powers of exposition, he does not know what he is saying?'[14]

But there is more to this story than simply an illustration of two clever people arguing – or rather, shouting – past one another. The two contestants struggling savagely in the cramped confines of *Philosophy*, like fig wasps fighting in the dark, were prefiguring much wider conflicts which became more urgent as the Darwinian reformation progressed and spread: what is it that Darwinism could usefully explain? And what consequences for humans followed from these explanations? Both questions have philosophical and bio-logical aspects; yet Midgley and Dawkins both argued as if the answers must be the same. This use of biology to answer philosophical questions is what has given Darwinism its peculiar resonance in pop science over the last twenty years. Dawkins the biologist failing to see that philosophy mattered and Midgley the philosopher misunderstanding his biology were among the first and most distinguished to use biology thus.

It has to be said that by the end of Dawkins's defence of his piece, which was published in *Philosophy* two years after Midgley's original offence, any impartial reader will see that she misunderstood him. But in the last paragraph he makes it quite clear that he has missed all her real points as

---

14 'Selfish Genes and Social Darwinism'.

thoroughly as she missed his.

'Midgley has a lot to say about metaphor and I can end constructively by explaining why it was unnecessary for her to say it. She thought I would defend my selfish genes by claiming that they were intended only as a metaphor, and assumed I was speaking metaphorically when I wrote, "We are survival machines – robot vehicles blindly programmed to preserve the selfish molecules known as genes. This is a truth that still fills me with astonishment." But that was no metaphor. I believe it is the literal truth, providing certain key words are defined in the particular ways favoured by biologists. Of course it is a hard truth to swallow at first gulp. As Dr Christopher Evans has remarked, "This horrendous concept – the total prostitution of all animal life, including Man and all his airs and graces, to the blind purposiveness of these minute virus-like substances – is so desperately at odds with almost every other view that Man has of himself that Dawkins' book has received a bleak reception in many quarters. Nevertheless, his argument is virtually irrefutable." '15

'The total prostitution of all animal life, including Man himself . . . to the blind purposiveness of these minute virus-like substances' is an odd phrase to quote if you are trying to clear yourself of the charge of genetic determinism. What is odder still is the nature of the authority that Dawkins was quoting to impress the readers of *Philosophy*: a pop science book of the time, *The Mighty Micro*, by Christopher Evans.16

---

15 Dawkins, 'In Defense of Selfish Genes', p. 573.

16 The sudden appearance of this unsolicited testimonial at the end of Dawkins's piece reminds me of a legendary concert review by an unprepared reporter. After four or five paragraphs of informed and technically perceptive praise, full of *scherzo*s and *legato*s and all cribbed from a friend, it concluded with one original line: 'The maestro was observed to play with equal facility on the black keys as on the white.'

This is one of those cheering works of technological boosterism which appeared a few years after the first micro-processors, to explain how much better computers would make everything. It predicted, for example, that the working week would be reduced to twenty-eight hours by the mid-Eighties, and that by the late Nineties we would none of us work more than twenty hours a week and all retire at fifty. Computers would make war impossible; and that they already exhibited genuine intelligence was taken as read.

It is an early illustration of the speed with which Dawkins's ideas appealed to the biologically unsophisticated reader, spread, and to some extent mutated as they did so. The analytical genes that Dawkins is interested in have one other important property as well as 'selfishness': they work like computer programs. The ribbon of DNA, with its digital information, and the tape on which computer programs used to be stored seem in some lights to be doing the same sort of job. The program tells the computer what to do; the DNA tells the cell what to do. This homology of analogies is strong stuff. It leads to the conclusion that an organism is just a computer which knows how to build another computer, and that DNA embodies that immortal, magical knowledge.

Immediately after the passage that Dawkins cites, Evans goes on to leap to this conclusion, and to illustrate its pitfalls. He starts to talk as if DNA provided a computer program that ran the whole organism, rather than just regulating cell development: 'Unfortunately [the selfish gene explanation] is also extremely simplistic, as the author himself agrees. It fails to acknowledge the significance and richness of the numerous *sub-goals* which are integral to and entirely supportive of the "main purpose", if one can call it that. These include . . . survival . . . mating and taking care of the young, eating and drinking, running away from some animals, and chasing others.'[17]

Yet the point of selfish gene theory is that the 'sub-goals' are all there are. The genetics of senescencè, as worked out by Sir Peter Medawar and William Hamilton, show that the survival of the individual is a goal that comes into direct conflict with the spread of the relevant genes. The genes win. Similar considerations apply to the other 'sub-goals' Evans lists. The male caddis fly, which mates after its head is bitten off, can hardly be said to have a harmonious relationship with its own sex drive.[18]

The deep confusion between 'selfish' as a moral term and 'selfish' meaning 'visible to a selection process' is further illustrated by one of the canonical triumphs of sociobiology, or selfish gene theory: David Haig's analysis of the relations between a mother and her foetus. Haig was a Harvard biologist who caught the excitement of selfish genery in the Eighties, and set out to analyse the relations between a mother and her foetus on the grounds that they could both be said to compete for the same resource: the mother's body.

This was an extension of Robert Trivers's original idea that there might well be genetically based conflicts of interest between parents and children in species where parents look after their young: it is to the genetic advantage of such a parent to have as many surviving children as possible, while it is to the advantage of each of those children to have as much parental care as possible at the expense of actual or even potential siblings. These two aims are usually compatible, but not identical.

The distinction between compatible and identical aims

---

17 *The Mighty Micro*, p. 17.
18 See Dawkins, *The Selfish Gene*, p. 5 and endnote (p. 268).

here, and the fact that they are so closely related, is another way of looking at the controversy over whether it is genes or bodies that are selected: for the purpose of analysing the different interests at stake, we can make a clear distinction between analytical genes in children and in parents. But of course these genes will actually be carried in the same body. If either gene should triumph, both would vanish.

Trivers was not arguing that there is a conflict between parents and their children in general – this is too obvious to remark on. The world is full of animal species in which mating is fatal, or at least the preliminary to death; human females, with their long infertile life after the menopause, are an exception to a very general rule.[19] What was subtle and gene-based about his argument was the definition of parental investment as the behaviour which benefits a child at the expense of its siblings, not at the expense of its parents. The genetic justification is that any given child has only a half of each parent's genes, on average.

But this form of theoretical conflict can be extended back into the womb. It might be expected to be even more intense there. More is at stake, after all: something like two-thirds of all naturally occurring human conceptions result in mis-carriages.[20] (Nor is animal reproduction much more efficient. This is an argument about mammals, not about humans specifically.) Most of these cases may be interpreted as the mother's body deciding that the foetus in question is a bad investment and flushing it in favour of a better bet. Since bear-ing healthy offspring who will themselves survive to repro-

---

19 For which there are further sociobiological explanations, involving gene–culture co-evolution.

20 The most common cause is egg-implantation failure, which often occurs so early in a pregnancy that the woman is unaware of having miscarried.

duce is the defining evolutionary aim of every mother, it is obvious that there must be selective pressure for such a skill.

That there would be selective pressure on a foetus not to be ejected and die is just as obvious. And to some extent, you would expect the foetus to do better in this contest – at least to be under greater pressure to win. It is a variant of the life/dinner principle, which explains why rabbits can almost always run faster than dogs: the rabbit is running for its life, and the dog is only running for a meal.

Some of the hormonal changes that a woman undergoes in pregnancy are explained in this way: for instance, a pregnant woman secretes more insulin than normally, which seems to be a response to the foetus secreting a hormone that neutralises maternal insulin: this has the effect of making more glucose available to the foetus in the mother's blood. The foetus is disrupting its mother's biochemistry for its own benefit, since the level of glucose which suits its purpose is rather higher than that which suits the mother. Of course, the process is entirely unconscious: indeed, one of the parties in this struggle is incapable of consciousness at all. The foetus does not always have the advantage: if the mother is not good at producing insulin, she may develop diabetes and even die, in which case everyone loses. But the odds are that this will not happen, and the foetus will benefit slightly. So selection maintains the struggle.

Similar reasoning has been applied by Haig to high maternal blood pressure, which can also develop into a life-threatening condition in pregnancy. The placenta, when it first forms, destroys those nerves and muscles in the mother which control the blood flow to the uterus. Any general raising of blood pressure in her body will then lead to an increased blood supply to the foetus; and the placenta (which is on the side of the foetus, not the mother, in this struggle) does secrete substances which constrict the mother's arteries.

The next step on this line of reasoning is to see the placenta itself as a foetal adaptation. The earliest mammals were all marsupials, whose young do most of their development in a handy external pouch. It is clearly to the benefit of the infant to spend time in a warm enclosed womb instead, plugged directly into its mother's bloodstream instead of having to rely on milk. One vivid description of the placenta from this point of view says: 'the fertilised egg is not content to hang around the uterus simply absorbing nutrition and waiting to be ejected a few weeks later. Instead it begins to behave like something out of a science fiction fantasy about a parasitic alien invader.'[21]

None the less, this story cannot be told simply in terms of a competition between the mother and the foetus. It could just as well be seen as a redistribution of resources within an animal's lifetime, so that more are allocated to the earliest period and fewer to a later one. Bearing larger and maturer young must be an adaptation which benefits the animal over its life as a whole, as embryo, mother, and grandmother, since placental mammals have driven the marsupials to extinction everywhere in the world except Australia.

The story of Haig's discovery is often told in the textbooks of selfish genery; yet, there, it often ends with the worrying tag line 'Even a mother's love is no longer sacred.' This is a classic example of confusing the two senses of selfishness. In the sense of selfish as 'visible to selection', there are clearly conflicts of interest possible between a mother and her children: Trivers and Haig have established this, and have shown some of the mechanisms by which the conflict expresses itself. But even in purely economic terms, when the

---

21 Elaine Morgan, *The Descent of the Child*, p. 18.

entire pattern is analysed as a competition for resources this conflict of interest is not absolute. If one side or the other gets all it bids for, both lose everything. It is more like mutually assured deterrence than a prisoner's dilemma.[22]

None of this, however, has anything to do with a mother's love of her children, whether this is viewed as an emotion or a moral obligation. For one thing, foetuses aren't children, and can't be loved in the same way. Miscarriages are horribly distressing, at least for humans, who can imagine where a pregnancy is leading. But they do not involve the same intensity of distress as the death of children. A mother's love, which is, in some ways, at least as much genetically programmed as her pregnancy, does not develop fully until the child is born and alive. To apply it to events in the womb is to make the same sort of error as the Roman Catholics who argue as if a foetus were a complete human being from the moment of conception.

---

22 'The prisoner's dilemma' is the name given to an exercise in game theory, in which there is no single best move: the best move in each turn of the game is dependent on what all the other players do. In its classic form, two prisoners are being interrogated separately. If neither confesses to the crime concerned, each will receive a short sentence for contempt of court. If one of them blames the other, the former will be released and the latter will get a heavy jail sentence; but if the two men blame each other, both will serve longer sentences than if both deny committing the crime. At first, it seems that the best move must always be to betray your accomplice. If he has kept loyally silent, you will be released; if he has betrayed you, your sentence will be shorter than if you have refused to co-operate with the authorities. But he can make the same calculation, so he will betray you back, and both of you will end up serving long sentences (though not the longest possible); whereas if both of you had kept silent, both would have had much shorter sentences. That is why it is called a dilemma: there are only two moves to choose from, and it is possible to prove that both are wrong.

The cellular struggles around the placenta are carried on without any conscious awareness on either side. They have no moral content. They do not involve feelings of either love or obligation. Talking as if they do is to ascribe agency and morality to things that can't have them. Sometimes this is harmless. Sometimes it is useful.[23] But when it is done in the context of a more general attempt to banish agency and morality from humans on the grounds that they are pre-scientific superstitions, this simply sweeps out seven devils to replace them with seventy-seven.

---

23 One perhaps underestimated explanation for the popularity of dramatic language in science is that it helps to explain to people why they should pay for the research.

6

PRIMITIVE COMBAT

ONE OF THE most controversial and elegant examples of adaptive reasoning was almost entirely unaffected by the disputes raging around the proper role and definition of a gene. In fact, the idea made its way almost outside the boundaries of professional biology, since the champion of the challenging idea was a middle-aged Welsh woman who had been one of the first successful writers for British television. But the 'aquatic ape theory' shows adaptationist reasoning in its most attractive light, since it seems to explain very clearly many of the puzzling things that distinguish us from chimpanzees and provides an evolutionarily plausible route from there to here.

When Elaine Morgan sold her first three television plays in the Fifties, she was working as a schoolteacher; she and her husband, Morien, had to go to a neighbour's house to watch the plays performed, since they had no television of their own. They were old-fashioned socialists from the mining valleys of South Wales. Morien had fought in the International Brigade in Spain; her proudest memory, she once wrote, was that she had once shared a speaker's platform with Bertrand Russell at a CND meeting.

With this background, you might have expected a

Gouldian. And it is true that she was drawn to evolutionary theory by a hostility to some of the early popularisers of evolutionary approaches to human nature, Robert Ardrey and Desmond Morris in particular. But she ended up defending a theory of human origins that was entirely adaptationist, and so duly described by Gould himself as 'claptrap'. Ardrey, in *African Genesis*, and Morris, in *The Naked Ape*, were not precursors of the sociobiologists in any rigorous sense: gene selection, reciprocal altruism, and game theory played no part in their reasoning. But both men wrote bestsellers which argued that the essentials of human nature could be deduced from the study of our origins, which is a project that obviously has a lot in common with sociobiology.

The nature they thought they had discovered was not a pleasant one. Ardrey popularised the idea that man had distinguished himself from his competing ancestors by savagery. Using palaeontological evidence now largely discredited he proposed that the species from which we descend had wiped out all its sibling species. In a striking example of the pseudo-religious imagery which was to become obligatory in popular science writing over the next decades, he proposed that we are the descendants of Cain, who had stolen Abel's land after killing him. As a serious account of human origins, this was about as reliable as *The Flintstones*; but for a while it was almost as popular, too. Suburban man wants to hear that deep down inside he is a rough, cruel killer – even if he would prefer those urges to stay buried except when he is safe inside a car.

The real crime of *Flintstones* anthropology is that it blurs and makes indistinct the problem which needs to be brought most sharply into focus: the fact that we are extraordinarily badly suited to survive without culture, if only in the form of tools and language, yet our physical form, which makes us so badly suited, seems to have appeared before our culture did. Our ancestors walked on two legs four or five million years ago while their brains were still small. Almost all the things that distinguish man from the apes have tended to make us less efficient than they are at living without tools or outside tribes. It is obvious from today's perspective that tools and tribes have enabled our species to rule the world. But natural selection has no foresight. Each change it approves has to make an immediate profit, and it is not clear how all the distinguishing business of humanity – being upright, hairless, and large-brained – could have profited our ancestors more than sticking to the traditional primate paths as chimpanzees did. There was nothing inevitable about the appearance of human beings.

In fact, Gould has argued that there is nothing inevitable about the appearance of any life form more complex than a bacterium, and that apparent dominance of the earth by multicellular life is only a trick perspective. Bacteria are not just overwhelmingly the most numerous organisms on earth (there are millions clinging to the unpromisingly sterile surface of my keyboard as I type); they may even be the dominant form measured by weight. If it were possible to weigh every living thing on earth, Gould argued in *Life's Grandeur*, then we might find that bacteria made up half the total weight of the biomass. Large size, complexity, purpose, and intelligence seem such important features of the world to us that it is easy and perhaps essential to overestimate their importance. But when J. B. S. Haldane was asked what natural selection could reveal of the nature of God, he pointed out that there are 400,000 species of beetle, but only 8,000 species of mammal; therefore 'The Creator, if He exists, has a special preference for beetles.'[1] The most successful animals on earth before we came along were insects and they have managed very well without intelligence or, mostly, tools.

So there is a general problem of complexity in evolution: why bother with all that multicellular complexity when you could be a bacterium? There is also the particular problem of why it should have suited a small ancestral ape to lose its hair and leave its safe trees for a life on the shelterless plains.

Morris, a trained zoologist, was less extravagant in his claims than Ardrey. Sex rather than violence seemed to him the most distinguishing mark of the human species. And it is true that rabbits would stand aghast, if they could, at the voracity and continuous nature of human sexual urges. Humans are almost unique in the animal kingdom in that they naturally find each other sexually interesting, even when there is no possibility of children resulting. This causes problems for all sorts of people, from the Pope downwards. But Ardrey and Morris had at least one thing in common: both wrote as if the central problem of human evolution was to explain the appearance of man, or of the men that book-buying men would like to be. This was what Elaine Morgan's first book set out to turn on its head in 1972. *The Descent of Woman* – the title is a throwback to Darwin's *The Descent of Man* – examined human anatomy from a feminist perspective. Instead of Man the Hunter, she was interested in Woman the Child-rearer. She wrote with style and pugnacious wit. The book sold hugely around the world and was translated into ten languages. It popularised a theory of

1 Lecture, 7 April 1951; report in *Journal of the British Interplanetary Society*, vol. 10 (1951), p. 156.

human origins which uses a purely adaptive approach to our anatomy.

The theory originated on a whaling ship in Antarctica in 1927, when a young Oxford zoologist, Alister Hardy, saw seals flayed. On his return to England, he was struck by a passage in a medical work which pointed out the way in which their fat layer clung to the skin, as it does in humans, rather than being attached to the body as it is in other animals. He began to wonder whether this fat layer in humans was an adaptation to an aquatic life. Hardy was a polymathic enthusiast. He invented a plankton-detector which, in widespread use, became, according to the *DNB*, 'the broadest and most regular ecological monitoring system in the world'. After leaving his post as Linacre Professor of Zoology in 1963, he founded a centre for the scientific study of religious experience, which attempted to set on a firm basis the widespread human sense of the numinous. And in 1960, when he was 65, he finally went public, with a lecture on his theory of aquatic evolution. After a brief flurry of interest ('Oxford Professor says man is a sea ape!') it was all but forgotten until Elaine Morgan came across it and tracked him down.

She developed the arguments increasingly over a period of about twenty years, working mostly without any collaboration from the academic world, at least until she discovered the Internet in her seventies. The things that the aquatic ape hypothesis sets out to explain are those which distinguish us from our ape relatives: hairlessness, bipedalism, speech, and our curious sexual habits, including face-to-face copulation.

All are explained on the hypothesis that they evolved in the almost weightless, dazzling, and relatively smell-less world of the seashore. In its developed form, the theory suggests that we descend from a population of apes which was trapped when its forested environment sank into the sea. This is supposed to have happened in what is now north-eastern Ethiopia, on the border with Eritrea. If such a population suddenly found itself on an island, all the conditions necessary for speciation would be met: it would be small, isolated, and under very strong pressure to evolve to cope with the changing conditions. The distinctively human anatomical features are then imagined as adaptations to life on the seashore.

The use to a wading animal of bipedalism is obvious; and there are monkeys living in flooded forests in Borneo which seem to be evolving this trait for very similar reasons. To be fatty and naked is also an adaptation which is only known among mammals which are, or have been, aquatic. There are other small indications that there may be connections between nakedness and an aquatic past. Hardy himself was much struck by the streamlined pattern in which hair grows on a newborn baby. The pattern of the hair roots corresponds exactly to the way in which water flows over a swimmer: inward at the shoulders, and then straight down the channel of the backbone. There is also the extremely bizarre fact that babies can swim before they can walk and seem reasonably comfortable with being born underwater.

What is less obvious is how useless habitual bipedalism is on the savannah or mosaic of forest and grassland where the conventional history has mankind evolving. Most apes can run much faster on four legs than on two. Much hunting is most efficiently done on no legs, slinking around as close to the ground as possible. If all you need to do is to stick your head up over the grass and look around to spot predators (or prey), this is something that chimpanzees can already do before dropping back on four feet to move. There is no need to walk on your back legs if all you want is to use them as an occasional viewing platform. Baboons live perfectly comfortably out there in the open scrub without feeling the need to walk on their hind legs.

A watery, wading life not only makes habitual bipedalism more sensible, for there will be advantages to wading slightly further out than your peers for most of the day; it also makes it easier. Bodies are lighter in water, fatty bodies especially so. Walking on her back legs must have been as painful and difficult to an ancestral ape as walking on all fours all day would be to us. It's possible: coal miners can spend their working days on all fours. But they do so because it is the only way to make a living; similarly pressing reasons must have operated to get our ancestors moving in the opposite direction. If their entire habitat were changing from a mountain range into a forested archipelago, as seems to have happened to the relevant bits of Ethiopia at about the right period, this would have supplied a reason much more cogent than simple curiosity about what was out there on the savannah.

Morgan also believes that bipedalism could have been maintained after we had returned to dry land by the loss of hair: human females offer their babies nothing to cling on to. Almost all other mammals, and certainly all other primates, are covered with hair that offers their young handholds, even footholds. A mother can move around quite freely and even forage without worrying about her baby. In humans, however, babies must be carried, so that a mother who wishes to move around with her baby must do so on two legs. This is a direct result of hairlessness, which would tend to reinforce bipedalism once it got started.

Fat insulation as opposed to hair is an adaptation found only in largish aquatic or swamp-dwelling mammals. Seals are about the largest hairy animals to make their homes in and around water. Above that size, hair seems to stop being a useful insulator; or at least its insulating merits are outweighed by its drawbacks. Walruses, pigs, and elephants are all largely hairless. Fat is useful even to hairy creatures like seals as an aid to streamlining. In that capacity, and as insulation, it makes sense to have fat distributed all over your body. If it is merely a store of energy, there is nothing wrong with concentrating it all in one place, usually a tail or a hump. Humans are not like that. Despite the paunches we grow with distressing ease, the rest of the body is usually fatty too. This makes dealing with heat much harder. Hair is popular among animals on the savannah partly because it is an excellent insulator and protects us from the sun. Morgan, following Darwin, believes that this drawback is so great that our hairlessness, once established by aquatic life, was maintained by sexual selection. It is difficult to think of any other mechanism which would cause only women to lose their beards, for their chins must once have been as thickly forested as men's.

The theory as originally developed by Alister Hardy dwelt on the anatomical features of man. Morgan extended it to cover our psychological characters to some extent. In this she was not completely alone. Hamilton made a sympathetic mention of her beliefs in the preface to one of his papers,[2] and added that he would expect that evolution on the shoreline would promote a more social disposition than would happen out in the savannah. The argument for this is that life on a shoreline, where each group has neighbours only to the left and right, rather than all around, makes intergroup hostility a little less likely, since it is more likely

---

2 'Innate Social Aptitudes of Man', pp. 340–1; also in conversation.

that neighbouring groups will share genes as a result of members transferring from one to another than it would be on a savannah where the choice of destinations is much wider. So far as I know, this is the only application of gene-centred analysis to the Aquatic Ape theory. All the rest of its arguments could have been made by Darwin, since they are dependent on the features of whole organisms.

For instance, there is the curious problem of language. It is obvious why we need language now. In fact, it is just about constitutive of a human being. The capacity to generate and understand language seems to be one of the functions of our brain which evolution has shaped and natural selection preserved. The benefits of language are so obvious that it is easy to fail to see the costs of evolving a spoken language. The difficulty with an adaptive explanation of language is not the question people used to ask about eyes – 'What use is half an eye?' – which has in any case been answered in principle by Richard Dawkins: 50 per cent of an eye will sometimes be importantly more useful than 49 per cent of an eye. This reasoning can be extended to cover any fraction of eyesight. It is always possible to imagine, and for an adaptationist, necessary to assume, circumstances in which a slightly more efficient eye makes a statistically noticeable difference to an animal's chances of reproductive success. The trouble with this explanation, when applied to human speech, is that apes already have half a language. They have a sophisticated communication system which uses smells, expressions, body language, and even noises to convey a lot of information about the outside world and about each other's state of mind. When chimps are offered non-verbal means of communication, such as plastic sign systems or computer keyboards, they seem to have a lot to say. But they cannot speak. They lack any fine-grained control over the noises they make.

The reasons for this inability are grossly anatomical. They are a matter not just of brain wiring, but of the way in which the larynx and the oesophagus of an ape, and indeed of most animals, are arranged. Humans can talk for the same anatomical reasons as they can choke to death: within six months of birth, the airways at the back of the mouth descend so that we can breathe through our mouths and control our breathing. This can hardly have evolved as a way to allow us to speak, argued Morgan, because it would violate the rule that all adaptations must show an immediate benefit. For natural selection to get somewhere, each succeeding change must show an incremental benefit over the preceding stage and the descent of our airways does not fulfil this criterion. The disadvantage of choking (and, perhaps, of Sudden Infant Death Syndrome) is immediate; the benefits of speech are long-term and require the simultaneous evolution of other faculties.

The only environment in which voluntary breath control offers an immediate advantage, outweighing the immediate disadvantages, is in the water. Aquatic mammals have all learnt to hold their breath. And, Morgan pointed out, they are also the animals which have made the most use of sound in communication. All methods of smell communication, which serve so well on land to indicate an animal's mood and territory, stop working in the sea for animals that must breathe air. If you want to escape a pack of pursuing dogs, cross running water. By the same token, if you want to communicate with them, stay away from the stuff. Primates are less smell-centred than most animals anyway, because they live in the trees, away from the ground to which scents cling. But human beings are quite remarkably insensitive to the news from their noses.

Similarly, she argued that the dazzle of the sea, combined with our increasingly fatty faces, would make facial expressions a less reliable form of communication, and tend to limit the range at which they were effective. Body language underwater is obviously much less subtle and visible than it is in the open air. All these factors would tend to put pressure on a social species to develop spoken language as a form of communication.

But the real impact of a loss of smell, it seemed to Morgan, was on women. They lost the ability to signal, through smell, when they were fertile and with that loss of oestrus came a host of troubles. The broken connection between sex and reproduction has done nearly as much as language to define the social world of human beings. Normally, in animals, a female is sexually attractive only when she is fertile. But in humans this is not the case. According to Morgan, this is a direct result of the loss of olfactory signals caused by a life lived in shallow water. So far as our instincts are concerned, sex has been detached from reproduction for as long as we have been human, certainly long before contraception made this detachment actual. This is such a central fact about human sexual instincts that its oddness by comparison with other animals is almost invisible. If I were looking for an evolutionary stimulus to the development of a moral sense, it is one of the places I would look, since it involves the necessary and continuously renewed clash of two powerful social instincts for parenting and sex – as the philosopher David Hull remarks, copulation is at least a minimally social activity.

This sociability seems increased by the human habit of copulating face to face. Indeed, this habit has been offered as an adaptation to make sex more sexy, and so more of a bonding mechanism. But as Morgan pointed out, making sex sexier does not necessarily make monogamy more attractive. She preferred to see this as another aquatic adaptation: one practised by almost all sea-going mammals, and very few others. It seems to arise from the straightening out of the spine and legs, which is also part of bipedalism.

Gould and Lewontin had both attacked the adaptationist programme for Panglossianism: supposing that whatever we find in organisms must be the product of efficient adaptation. But the arguments of the aquatic ape theory, as developed by Morgan, hinged crucially on how badly adapted we are in a simple physical sense to our present life as bipeds, and specifically on how badly adapted women are. This may seem a mere inversion of the *Flintstones* fantasy that we are really well adapted to be roaring beasts of the savannah. It may have started off as that. But as her arguments progressed, they cut deeper. One of her later books was called *The Scars of Evolution*. She argued more and more from the wrongnesses and the costs of human adaptations, compared to those of chimpanzees. Her motto might have been the punchline of the old Irish joke: 'If I were going to there, I wouldn't start from here.'

At the same time, there is some evidence that a diet of seafood, crustacea and so on would be good for the brain. They contain in high concentrations a form of oil which is essential to the development of brain cells; and there is a theory that this diet helped to set our brains on their path to world domination.

So the aquatic ape theory is one of the most powerful and attractive examples of adaptive thinking around, not least because it provides a single answer to a multitude of apparently unrelated problems. This is unusual. The normal problem with adaptive explanations is that there are too many of them for any particular problem. None the less, it has been resisted in almost every particular by palaeontologists, and this is worth looking at, too.

There are bad reasons for this. As Morgan told me, 'The undergraduates believe my theory, so the professors assume it must be wrong.' But there are also solid reasons for doubting the hypothesis, beautiful though it is. In detail, a lot of the assertions about the uniquely naked, fatty character of human beings seem to break down. Lots of aquatic animals have kept their fur, especially those as small as our aquatic ancestor is supposed to have been: Lucy, the first upright hominid fossil found, was only about four feet tall, and she must, *ex hypothesi*, have been post-aquatic. The distribution of fat on human bodies is not terribly insulating; rather, it appears to be a store of energy, perhaps even a form of streamlining. This is especially apparent when you consider the ways in which the fat is broken down: the first fat to be consumed by a hungry body is the insulating and streamlining layer over the upper body; the last to go is the useless lump over the belly.

It is true that babies know not to breathe when plunged underwater; and that humans also have or can develop a diving reflex which slows down their heart rate considerably when they are long submerged. But we also have a strikingly non-adaptive feature for aquatic life: we drown. Humans, like apes but unlike monkeys and almost all other animals, including such hydrophobic beasts as cats, drown readily unless they have been taught to swim; and it has been argued that this knowledge, being cultural, could not have been transmitted by creatures with such small brains as our aquatic ancestors had.[3]

There are even arguments about bipedalism, apparently

---

3 Jan Wind, *The Aquatic Ape: Fact or Fiction?*

the strongest part of the aquatic argument. A wading life would undoubtedly have made it much easier and more profitable to stand upright; but the most efficient form of locomotion in the water is to have legs that are much longer below the knee than above it. This adaptation may be seen in wading birds; it is not found in humans, or in any hominid fossils. There is, in fact, a link between bipedalism and a susceptibility to drowning: an animal used to walking on all fours is likely to have its nose and eyes above water because they sit on top of its body: a human, lying flat in the water to swim, must flex his neck backwards or twist it sideways to breathe, as anyone knows who has done the breast stroke or the crawl.

Finally, there is the problem of time. When is the aquatic stage supposed to have happened? Alister Hardy's original estimate, made in 1960, was that it would have required perhaps 10 million years for the necessary modifications to be made. These 10 million years are nowhere to be found in the fossil record. The window for aquatic modifications seems to have shrunk to 1 or 2 million years, around 5 million years ago. It does not help that the supposed site of the aquatic period is to be found in one of the most desolate and frequently fought over parts of Africa, on the borders of Ethiopia and Eritrea. For most of the last thirty years, it would have been impossible for anyone to go fossicking about there in search of evidence for a theory of human origins.

Whether it would be possible to find fossil evidence of hairlessness, relative fattiness, or even of aquatic adaptations, and so settle the matter, is another question. It is probable that the question will remain undecided for ever. Yet this is, as I have said, one of the most attractive of all the adaptive accounts of biological history. The fact that adaptive explanations can be generated for both sides of the argument, and to cover all the points in dispute, either by changing the definition of the feature being adapted, or by pointing to other possible uses, suggests some of the frustrations and swamps into which a general faith in adaptation can lead people when they try to apply it.

Another illustration of the difficulties of adaptationist explanations of human nature is provided by the case of the Yanomamo. There are fashions in noble savages as in other things, and the Yanomamo, a warlike and intermittently cannibal tribe living on the borders of Brazil and Venezuela, were in the Seventies and Eighties one of the most heavily studied and nastiest in their habits of all the unspoiled peoples left. Yet two quite different adaptationist explanations of their behaviour were put forward.

The tribe is exceptionally violent and sexist. The Yanomamo term for marriage translates literally as 'dragging something away'; their term for divorce is 'throwing something away'. Villages war with villages; villagers with each other. They use poisoned arrows, spears and wooden clubs. When nothing much seems to be happening in the world outside, villagers fight with long poles. Two men stand facing each other, and exchange insults. Then they take turns to punch each other in the chest as hard as possible. Finally they take up long flexible poles, and – once more taking turns – smash each other round the head with them until the loser is felled, unconscious and bleeding all over his head. To quote one lurid description: 'A man with a special grudge against another challenges his adversary to hit him on the head with an eight foot long pole shaped like a pool cue. The challenger sticks his own pole in the ground, leans on it, and bows his head. His adversary holds his pole by the thin end, whipping the heavy end down on the proffered pate with bone-crushing force. Having sustained one blow, the recipient is entitled to an immediate opportunity to wallop his opponent in the same manner.'[4]

There is nothing quite like this outside the correspondence columns of the *New York Review of Books*.

Yet what is the point of it all? Why do the Yanomamo behave as they do? There are two broad answers proposed, by Napoleon Chagnon, an anthropologist who has spent much of his life studying them, and a rival interpretation by Marvin Harris, another anthropologist, who seems to have spent much of his life studying Chagnon's results. For Harris, the explanation is reasonably simple. The selection takes place at a cultural level, independently of the instincts of the men involved. What keeps the Yanomamo hitting and killing each other, year after year, is that this behaviour brings tangible benefits to them or to their villages. Specifically, Harris believes that the condition of constant warfare keeps the population sparse and the villages widely separated, which in turn ensures that the game is not hunted to extinction. A well-armed Yanomamo village in rude health acts as a sort of game warden, ensuring that no one else can hunt on its patch. This in turn keeps the density of the game high, which keeps the villagers well fed, which enables them to defend their patch. And so the cycle goes on.

Harris made something of a career analysing cultural practices in terms of their utility to the cultures that practised them. Perhaps the most impressive was his story about the sacred cows of India. These have always been to Westerners a byword for the superstitious waste of resources. They are never killed, no matter how much of a nuisance they may

---

4 Marvin Harris, *Cows, Pigs, Wars and Witches*, pp. 71ff.

be, no matter what they eat, and no matter how hungry their worshippers are. And when you visit a Hindu temple in Hertfordshire, and are shown the herd of Jersey cows by a saffron-robed monk with a strong Belfast accent, who is convinced that by keeping these cattle on some of the most luscious grass in the world he is pleasing the Gods and making the world a better place, it is easy to conclude that the whole thing is irrational beyond words, if not quite beyond belief.

This conclusion may be rash. When the reverence for cows is examined on its native soil it turns out to have some profoundly rational grounds. The soil is the key to Harris's argument, for the bullocks that Hindus so revere are the only animals mostly used for ploughing it. This means that, even in a drought, eating your cows is an admission of utter defeat. When the rains return, if you have no draught animals, you will starve anyway, or be compelled to sell yourself into slavery. To eat the beast that pulls your plough is the functional equivalent of eating the seed corn. It may well happen in times of extreme famine, but so does cannibalism. In any normal conditions, including those of 'normal' famine, cows are safe, and keeping them safe also represents the best policy. Of course, the presence of a strong tabu helps to preserve them, but the tabu would wither if it were not also profitable. Besides, he points out, dead cows are eaten anyway, providing they have died of natural causes, and while they wander around unmolested they also perform an important economic service when they eat – at least indirectly – for their dung is the basic fuel on the treeless plains of north India.

In the end, for Harris, and the mainstream anthropological tradition that he represents, cows are sacred not because there is any deep universal human drive to revere cattle, nor because human beings are fundamentally irrational, but because the tabu benefits the societies that practise it; and when it stops making sense, it will be dropped.

Perhaps the most impressive form of this analysis came when he considered the savagery of the Aztecs. Again, this looks like one of the classic examples of an evil and cruel religion. Evil and cruel it undoubtedly was. But in the circumstances of Mexico before the Europeans came, it may have made economic sense to sacrifice hundreds of prisoners of war a day. The method was gory. The prisoners were marched to the top of a pyramid, spreadeagled over an altar stone, and then had their chests hacked open with an obsidian knife. The heart was pulled out, still beating if the prisoner had survived the operation, and held up to the sun. The bodies were then tumbled down the pyramid, and later eaten. It is in this last fact that Harris finds the secret of the practice. For twenty thousand prisoners a year supply an awful lot of protein; and in Central America under the Aztecs, there was no meat-bearing animal larger than a guinea-pig.[5]

The sacrificed prisoners were the property of the warriors who had captured them; and their bodies were served up at banquets, which served also to enhance the status of the banquet giver. The arrangement gave a successful warrior status and nourishment all at once, along with a really powerful incentive to avoid capture himself: it's easy to see how a society with these practices could be triumphant in

---

5 This in itself may have been due to human intervention. The evidence is strong that the large animals native to the Americas before any humans arrived were all exterminated by man as the first American tribes moved across the continent.

hand to hand warfare over its neighbours; and this fact seems to Harris to explain satisfactorily how human sacrifice could persist for two hundred years until the Aztecs came up against the scarcely more gentle, but much better armed and fed, conquistadors.

This kind of reasoning dwells entirely on the benefits to the societies involved of the practices being analysed. It assumes that human nature is almost infinitely malleable. Though some historians have compared the Aztecs to the Inquisition, as if there were little to choose between the two religions, this is more a reflection of nineteenth-century American anti-Catholic prejudice than anything based on a serious comparison of the amount of suffering caused. (And when the Aztecs are compared with most other cultures, their bloodlust is extraordinary.) Human nature, to this school of anthropologists, can adapt itself to almost anything, from strict vegetarianism to a diet of regular human flesh supplements. It can adapt to almost every imaginable sexual arrangement except, perhaps, pure matriarchy.

This diversity seems to prove that all these cultural adaptations cannot be reduced to psychology, any more than psychology can be reduced to chemistry. This was a conclusion reached in the very early years of anthropology as a discipline, when Darwinism also first got going. The problem was, as so often, that adaptive explanations were just too powerful. They could explain anything. If they are, in Daniel Dennett's phrase, 'a universal acid', capable of eating through everything, they will eventually consume even the subjects we want them to illuminate. It's not much use having a magic substance that will unblock your intellectual drains if it eats out the bottom of the sink as well.

As the distinguished anthropologist Maurice Bloch remarked at a Darwin Seminar at the LSE: 'The main theoretical teaching we pass on to our students is that it is rude to try to explain anything. Given that state of affairs it is not surprising that the general public is not thrilled. [But] Wilson, Dawkins, and Pinker are [only] able to satisfy their public so readily because they do not understand the problems which led anthropologists to withdraw from the field.'[6]

These problems are twofold. First, adaptationism can explain any conceivable human behaviour – and then explain its opposite just as well: 'As Pinker shows, you can explain the universality of romantic love in terms of gene fitness; you can also explain the irrelevance of romantic love in terms of fitness.'[7]

The second point is that social patterns are embedded in a complex web of social meanings even when they are founded on instinct. Marriage is more than copulation; even primitive war is more than random murder; food tabus are not simple expressions of disgust: 'Pinker tells us human beings universally find some things disgusting, and I would agree. But what has that to do with tabu foods?'[8]

To argue that anthropology must be conducted as if there were no such thing as human nature is not the same as arguing that no such nature actually exists. But the social sciences, throughout the Sixties and much of the Seventies, were conducted as if the two positions were the same; and as if anthropology had proved that human nature was an illusion.

There are some sociobiologists who are convinced that

---

6 The seminar was held on 12 February 1988; the contributions were not published.

7 Ibid.

8 Ibid.

they can still discern the innate scaffoldings of the human personality, if they specify clearly enough the problems they believe our minds and emotions are adapted to solve. These people became the founders of a successor discipline to sociobiology, known as 'evolutionary psychology'; and one of them was Napoleon Chagnon, the ethnologist whose descriptions of the Yanomamo Marvin Harris used to support his own diametrically opposed theories.

7

SOCIOBIOLOGY RESURGENT

CHAGNON ARGUES THAT the Yanomamo are satisfying primal human urges rather than secondary, cultural or economic ones. Their societies evolved not to compete with other Yanomamo societies, but to spread the genes of the winners. He argues against Harris that the motive force of Yanomamo violence is not competition for resources, at least not directly. Instead, he understands it as competition between kin groups. The ferocity is the point, and the ecological benefits the by-products. Neither party to this argument considers a third possibility: that this ferocity might have arisen as a result of competing social strategies within villages, rather than between villages.

Chagnon's position is deeply controversial in all sorts of ways: for one thing, the Yanomamo, since their discovery in the late Sixties, and their first description by Chagnon, have become the victims of a gold-rush around the headwaters of the Orinoco. Their lands have been stolen, some of them have been massacred by miners, and they have suffered dreadfully from imported diseases. This has led to their reinvention as cuddly endangered savages, with conse-quences that are partly ludicrous. You can even buy a children's book about their lives in the unspoilt rainforest.

The publishers say, 'This stunning photo-essay follows the lives of the Yanomamo people in their daily routine – hunting, fishing and playing – giving children a glimpse of the lives of a vanishing people. This will teach children to respect the ways of another culture and perhaps even to help it survive.'

The two most famous images of the Yanomamo in early films made by Chagnon show the sudden outbreak of a mass axe-fight, and a group of warriors getting a hallucinogenic powder blown up their noses by a shaman, after which they reel to the nearest upright post, hang on to it with both hands, and vomit. If these are the inhabitants of Eden, the anthropologists reached them millennia after the serpent.

There is a further irony in this reinvention of the Yanomamo as Edenic. The Westerners who see them as noble and the Westerners who see in them only savages actually agree on one fundamental point: that primitive people are closer to their real nature than we are. Chagnon would argue that under the skin we are all Yanomamo. This is not because the sociobiologists – Dawkinsians – believe that primitive tribes have less culture, or a less culturally mediated experience of the world than we have: what they believe is that our emotions have evolved to deal with the culture of a Stone Age tribe.

This argument depends on two steps: the first is that the Yanomamo behaviour is best understood by aggregating their individual urges. They do not act because they are moulded by their culture: their culture is merely the sum of their acts. The second is that for most of human history we evolved in societies rather like those of Stone Age tribes today, where there were no social bonds tighter than kinship, and the largest villages or groups might have two hundred inhabitants. Very high rates of homicide are reported from such primitive populations all around the world. A 1995 study,[1] quoted by Chagnon,[2] gave some astonishing cross-cultural figures. The homicide rate in modern Britain is roughly 0.5 in 100,000; in the USA it is about twenty times as high, at about 10.5. The highest death rate recorded in a nation, as opposed to a tribe, is 34 in 100,000, in Colombia. Though it is difficult to calculate exact correspondences for much smaller populations, about whom much less is known, it is still clear that Stone Age tribes make up in enthusiasm what they lack in the technology of murder. Even the !Kung bushmen, popularised as 'The Harmless People', had a homicide rate of 41.9 on this scale; the Yanomamo come in at 165. In the study the record was held by the Hewa people of New Guinea, with a score of 778.[3]

There are problems with these figures. None of the societies studied is, or could be, wholly unspoiled or unaffected by the distant presence of the Western cultures whose representatives study them. The Yanomamo even have a few metal implements, traded in from the distant coasts, and one theory about their war-making is that it is all really about the acquisition of these tools. More importantly, their entire economy is based on bananas and plantains, both plants which have diffused to the region as a result of European settlement elsewhere in South America. It is probably true that the invention of agriculture has changed every ecosystem where man can live in the last ten thousand years,

---

1 CIBA Foundation, *The Genetics of Criminal and Anti-social Behaviour.*
2 Chagnon, CIBA Foundation.
3 Chagnon has a chart and discussion of these figures, which are taken from pp. 214–17 of CIBA; they come originally from Professor Bruce Knauft's 1987 paper 'Reconsidering Violence in Simple Human Societies'.

even among those tribes who do not practise it. It is possible to argue that hunter-gatherers are not as violent as agriculturalists, though the Murngin hunter-gatherer aborigines of Northern Australia come in with a score of 330.

Chagnon argues that the essential fact about these societies is not their technology but their social structure, in which everything is based around kinship groups. If Stone Age tribes today are close to the social environment in which humanity and its immediate ancestors have lived for most of the past hundred thousand years, you would expect us to have evolved some traits to cope with an environment in which being killed by your fellows was a notable statistical risk. He believes that we have an emotional adaptation to violence in certain circumstances. This is not the same as supposing that there is such a thing as a quota or reservoir of aggression inside everyone. It also has very little to do with the circumstances of modern war. The argument is at least partly about whether people can discover, under certain circumstances, that they enjoy violence and the infliction of pain and fear. Chagnon has taken an anthropological route to the conclusion that Hamilton thought he had discovered by introspection and which Price intuited by mathematics.

It's hard to see how it could have been controversial to anyone at the end of this century that human beings can take pleasure in the infliction of pain and in the extermination of their fellows. Yet the subject is still largely tabu when it is conjoined with adaptationism. To argue that the emotional reactions to which human beings are subject are those which would have tended to maximise reproductive success on the savannah where we are supposed to have evolved really does assert that decency has no intrinsic value and is something the human race could grow out of if it stopped being useful.

One way out of the dilemma, taken by George Williams,

the man who defined the analytical gene, is to argue that there may have been many different environments of evolutionary adaptation: this would mean that not one but a wide variety of social strategies and responses could have become genetically fixed as we evolved on the savannah.[4] He is a giant in his field, so what he proposes must, genetically, be possible. But his solution raises a great many new questions. What happened to all these different genetically programmed strategies? Are they preserved among different races or populations, or did they at some stage mix into a common pool, yet still preserve their individuality? And, if they did, would not one or two of them triumph over the others, and restore a common nature to the human race? There may be answers to all these questions. But it is difficult to think of any that would not destroy the hopes of sociobiology to provide a single unified account of the social adaptations that make us human.

It is more or less taken for granted that many of these adaptations are actively harmful in a modern civilised environment. If you want to find people who actually behave like the Yanomamo in the modern world, you must look at Hell's Angels or other gang members. This is one reason why the whole subject is hugely controversial. In 1995, when the eminently respectable CIBA Foundation held a seminar in London on 'The Genetics of Criminal and Anti-social Behaviour', the whole thing was kept as secret as possible, and none of the participants would talk to the press at all, though at other seminars in the same series house-trained journalists were permitted to sit in a corner and watch. The papers and discussions of the seminar were published that year, and show how remarkably sophisticated

4 See George Williams and Randy Nessé, *Evolution and Healing*, pp. 138ff.

the field has become after twenty years of almost continuous criticism.

For one thing, Martin Daly, a psychologist who represented Chagnon at the conference, made it clear that he was not interested in individual variations in violent behaviour. He distinguished between two fields of study: behavioural genetics and EMABS, an unlovely acronym for the clumsily named 'evolution-minded adaptationist behavioural science'. These two jargon terms turn out to map neatly onto the distinction between analytic and functional genes as they affect behaviour. Behavioural genetics studies functional genes, and looks for particular ways in which changes at the level of DNA will cause brains to grow in particular ways that may lead to violence, madness or, indeed, their opposites. Daly's EMABS studies analytic genes, and asks what kind of behaviours could be expected to appear as abstract adaptations. Then he goes looking for them.

He and his wife, Margo Wilson, produced one of the founding successes of evolutionary psychology: the discovery that people murder their stepchildren a hundred times more often than they murder their own. This is shocking and they are shocked by it; though not, perhaps, as shocked as their opponents. What their figures appear to show is that when the figures for homicide in any country with reliable statistics are collected, most murdered children are killed by their step-parents. What is more, when biological parents kill their children, they tend to do so as painlessly as possible. Homicidal step-parents, on the other hand, are usually violent and sometimes deliberately cruel.

Daly and Wilson's research says nothing about the mechanisms that may have produced these effects. They have not studied live step-parents at all, but have relied on statistics. Their research was hampered for years by the fact that no one kept statistics, when children were murdered by their parents, which recorded whether these were biological or step-parents. There are some scientists who still mutter about the figures, but they are generally accepted.

One need not postulate a baboon-like strategy of killing all your mate's children by another man to get the Cinderella effect: all that would be necessary is a slight diminution, when applied to other children, of the inhibitions that stop us killing our own children, despite all the provocation they offer. That's easy to believe in without committing yourself to a view of human nature as limitlessly depraved and callous.

If you were the sort of man who regularly hit children, including his own, when they irritated him, it seems plausible that you would have slightly greater inhibitions about beating your own up than about beating other people's. Remember, these crimes are not usually deliberate murder so much as beating or bullying gone too far. Remember, too, how unbearable a whingey baby can be. There's not a parent in the world who has not had to put one down and leave it in another room while he or she gains control. Some adults are less good at that than others (for reasons which may have a genetic component, though that is irrelevant to this argument). However the temptation arises, all Daly and Wilson's arguments require is a slightly greater resistance to temptation when it is supplied by family members rather than strangers. Intuitively, that seems right. If I ran a child over and killed it, I would feel dreadful for the rest of my life. If I ran my own daughter over, I don't know how I could avoid suicide. That is, among other things, a measure of the differing values I feel their lives have.

So I can believe Daly and Wilson, if the statistics stand up, without thereby feeling that my view of the human race and its possibilities is much darkened. Nothing of theirs compares for horror with a throwaway line in an article that a friend of mine once wrote about an elderly Belorussian living out his days in a suburb of Birmingham after an energetic war spent helping the SS kill Jews. This man was on very good terms with his stepson: indeed, when they went for walks together he would sometimes show him, with gestures, the correct way to dash out a baby's brains against a wall. Who needs genetics when you have cultural transmission?

Of course this question is slightly misleading, because genetic and cultural transmissions are not alternatives but both necessary. If it were not possible for humans under some circumstances to learn the skill of baby-braining, there would be no point in trying to teach them. But if it came as naturally as walking, there would be no need to teach it.

It is important to realise that Daly and Wilson are agnostic as to the precise mechanisms, the functional genes and their interaction with the environment, which lead to their results. They are interested in analytical genes. '[Our] theory and research are overwhelmingly focussed on predicting and explaining the detailed nature of environmental, not genetic, sources of behaviour variation.'[5]

They analyse, in other words, abstract relationships between social actors, such as mates, parents and their children, or unrelated adults. The theories they come up with are then tested against statistical results. For example, they claim that unrelated men are more likely to kill each other if they stand to gain by it, and their chance of gaining status by such an act varies according to whether they are married, whether they have a stake in society, and what their

---

5 CIBA, p. 186.

life expectancy and prospects are.[6] Desperate men are dangerous. This may not seem a tremendous scientific breakthrough, but there are a couple of very important things to note about their predictions. The first is that they do not claim that anyone makes calculations of this sort. On the contrary, the assumption is that murders are committed for all the emotional reasons we already know: rage, despair, fear, whatever. The argument is that our propensity to feel these connections is itself governed by a deeper logic and shaped by adaptation. It is no more than a propensity. The emotions emerge only in the statistical analysis of thousands of cases. In any individual case there will always be a whole complex play of motive and opportunity, history and contingency. But, they claim, our natures are such that under certain pressures we will buckle in certain ways, which can be successfully predicted by an abstract consideration of the ways in which genes flow.

Daly and Wilson believe that these abstract principles enable them to predict the emergence of patriarchy, male jealousy, and even a tendency to see newborn babies as more closely resembling their fathers than their mothers as well as a disproportionate infliction of violence on stepchildren. The argument about who newborn babies look like is based on the idea that fathers will want to invest time and care only in the children they believe are their own. This disposition is produced by purely Hamilton motives: only if an apparently altruistic act benefits other copies of the genes that cause it to be performed will it become established in a population. So, if women want their children to be looked after, it is in their interest to convince their mates that they are in fact the fathers. One way of doing so is to detect a

---

6 Ibid.

resemblance between the newborn and its father. A study of videotaped births in an American hospital revealed that mothers were indeed far keener than fathers to spot a resemblance; though a subsequent, larger study in Canada provided ambiguous evidence.

Both adaptationists and their enemies would agree that you can get a long way starting from bollocks. George Williams, who coined the term 'the adaptationist programme', uses the position of the human testicles as a beautiful example of adaptationist reasoning: the ducts which lead from them to the penis are looped inside the body over other tubes. This is a ludicrous arrangement, which can be explained only on the grounds that the testicles must originally have been positioned inside the body and only slowly have descended. Their plumbing is a type example of the adaptationist argument from apparent maladaptation. Daly and Wilson, meanwhile, deduce lasting characteristics of female sexuality from the size of human testicles rather than from their position. Relative to body size, men's are much larger than gorillas'. However, they are much smaller, relatively speaking, than those of the chimpanzee. The difference is to be explained by utility. Gorillas are completely patriarchal. For them it is absolutely true that men are polygamous, women monogamous. The relatively large testicles of chimpanzees are a consequence of greater female sexual freedom. The male reproductive strategy, they argue, involves 'sperm competition' – producing as much of the stuff as possible in the hope that it will not only reach the egg first, but serve, by its presence, to keep the sperm of rival males away. Even the scrotum is understood as an adaptation to the problem of having fertile sperm readily available, at the price of a certain vulnerability compared to those animals, like gorillas, which keep their testicles tucked safely, but less productively, in their bodies.

Wilson and Daly argue that the possessiveness and tendency to violence which, traditionally, distinguish human males, can be predicted by evolutionary logic. In a species in which females are not strictly monogamous and males are as little monogamous as they can get away with, certain characteristics, such as jealousy, can be expected to evolve. They offer no explanation as to why some primates should mate like bonobo chimpanzees – with everyone, all the time – and others like gorillas. But, they say, given the mating patterns of our species while it was evolving, you would expect to find men treating, and understanding, women as property simply because they are women.

Adultery, they claim, is in almost all cultures defined as the alienation of a man's property. They claim to have found evidence from law codes in all sorts of countries and cultures to support a view of adultery as a crime women commit, by acting in a way which makes the fatherhood of their children dubious. 'Men take a proprietary view of women's sexuality and reproductive capacity . . . They lay claim to particular women as songbirds lay claim to territories, as lions lay claim to a kill, or as people of both sexes lay claim to valuables. Having located an individually recognisable and potentially defensible resource packet, the proprietary creature proceeds to advertise and exercise the intention of defending it from rivals . . . We argue that sexually proprietary male psychologies are evolved solutions to the adaptive problems of male reproductive competition and the potential misdirection of paternal investments in species with mistakable paternity.'[7]

Their argument proceeds in two steps. The first is the

---

7 'The Man who Mistook his Wife for a Chattel'.

extraction of formal patterns, or games, played by such actors as mates, rivals, and parents and children. This descends from the game-theoretical work done by Price and Maynard Smith. The second is to identify such patterns in the real world.

Because they are looking for archetypal behaviours, which have already been fixed as clearly advantageous by selection, individual variations, on which selection might now be acting in a different direction, do not interest them: 'Constitutional differences among individuals are not what is at issue, and are ignored, either washed out statistically or treated as "noise".'[8] Of course, the argument goes, there must have been variability in the past; but if we have correctly identified essential features of any gene-based morality, they will long since have been established in the population.

This is especially germane to the discussion of whether war is an innate human activity, for all the evidence suggests that modern war is something we are not very good at. Technological war makes it possible, even for those with remarkably little aptitude for the business, to kill people. But all the studies done on how men actually behave in battle show that only a tiny minority really flourish there. Killing people is a learned skill, though we may have an innate aptitude to learn it; and the willingness and capacity to learn is very variable. Studies of sets of twins who fought in the Vietnam war indicate that there is a strong genetic influence on whether people are wounded, and whether they win medals. This makes no sense until you realise that being wounded in a modern war is not always, perhaps not often, a completely random experience. A battlefield is full of

---

8 CIBA, p. 186.

differing risks, which an experienced soldier will recognise: that's what makes him experienced; and a willingness to take certain sorts of risks in certain circumstances seems to be influenced by mood and temperament. Robert Graves, for example, describing his experiences on the Western Front in *Goodbye to All That*, has a passage explaining how he would take certain short cuts through the trench system only when very tired, because he estimated the risk of getting hit at one in nine, whereas on his normal route the risk was only one in fifteen. But when he heard that his friend Siegfried Sassoon had been wounded, in his misery and frustration he started ignoring these calculations and taking greater and greater risks, until eventually he won a medal.

The strong genetic variability which studies of twins suggest actually argues against homicidal violence being the basic way in which human males approach each other. For if it were more advantageous to be a good fighter than anything else, this capacity would have been strongly developed by natural selection until all the alternate strategies had died out. Daly and Wilson's arguments about human nature being bad news for stepchildren also suggest, paradoxically, that human nature is good news for pacifists, since the war-making instincts still vary so much within populations.

Primitive war differs from modern war in all sorts of ways, but primarily by being a social activity undertaken for personal motives. The Trojan War was fought over a woman, but also over honour. Chagnon and Daly believe that honour is much more important than women in the conduct of primitive wars, and that revenge is the most important motive of all. Primitive wars are in essence vendettas, in which two extended families with a history of killing each other add to that history. Yet vendettas can end.

Daly summed up the implications of Chagnon's arguments by saying that 'The capacity for violence, and the capacity to use it when the situation demands, is certainly not a pathology. It is probably an organised attribute of human nature as a result of selective consequences in pre-state societies, in which men who were capable in violent situations did well. Therefore we have got to think in terms of an evolved capacity for modulated violence.'[9]

But, he went on to say, this is not fixed. It is a capacity, which can be unlearnt, even by people who have grown up in societies where homicidal behaviour is the norm. Among the Yanomamo, there is far more killing in the fertile river basins near the Orinoco, where the land is most desirable, than there is in the highlands to which dispossessed tribes have moved, where the living is harsher. Daly told the CIBA seminar: 'The cases where people who have immigrated after defeat from the lowlands and adopted a different lifestyle illustrate that even within the lifespan of a person raised in a society in which there is a strong social valuation of violent capacity . . . people are well capable of laying off violence.'[10]

So the search for innate human capacities ends up by rediscovering the importance of social factors, and of the environment. This is important, because the more stupid supporters and the more intelligent opponents of the Dawkinsian programme tend to see it in terms of a genetic determinism which, when you get down to the nitty-gritty, just isn't there. It's easy enough to show the inadequacies of traditional anthropological explanations. As one recent study of the origins of war concluded: 'The cultural determinists

---

9 CIBA, p. 235.
10 Ibid.

were highly sceptical about so-called laws of behaviour which might limit the power and autonomy of culture. They especially did not believe that warfare performed any regular functions either proximate or grand. They tended to describe warfare (if they did at all, for mostly they preferred to ignore it, which is why I have not attempted to identify this thesis with any one author) as a relatively superficial adaptation or maladaptation, with the implication that it might easily be got rid of. [The anthropologist] Margaret Mead made this explicit in a 1940 essay entitled "War is Only an Invention – Not a Biological Necessity" in which she argued that warfare is a "historical accident" persisted in (apparently) from force of habit. She admitted that primitive warfare served a variety of purposes, but to her that seemed to establish its superficiality.'[11]

But what one is left with when cultural determinism is defeated is not a genetic determinism. It is a complex mixture of interacting factors, in which different rules clash and produce a limited freedom.

If that is in fact the world we live in, it begins to make sense that Darwinian processes should have produced at least one animal to whom it is advantageous to have a mind capable of recognising and even defining abstract things like freedom. And while part of evolutionary psychology deals with the origin of human emotions, another branch deals with the origin of human intellectual powers, though one of the leitmotifs of both branches is that the division is not clear: intellect, emotion, and self-interest are all inextricably twined together in mutual development.

The two pioneers of the second branch, in the 1980s, were John Tooby and Leda Cosmides, psychologists who

---

11 Doyne Dawson, 'The Origins of War'.

had been studying at Harvard when Wilson's original *Sociobiology* came out. With them, one circle from computers to genetics is completed: Hamilton and Price started out using computers to discover how minds might have evolved. For Tooby and Cosmides, computers are what nature has produced in human brains. Our minds, they say, are computers, though made of carbon not silicon. This is not a view popular among neuroscientists, to whom the differences between brains and computers are obvious.[12] But the metaphor of brains as, in the last analysis, information-processing devices is very popular among Dawkinsians, who always describe the brain as processing information, rather than use alternatives such as 'finding meaning'.

Yet meaning is only information with necessary consequences, and few animals apart from ourselves seem complex enough to enjoy information for its own sake, without practical consequences. Tooby and Cosmides's research aims to show that our minds are designed to find particular meanings in the world around us, or, as they would have it, to process information in particular ways. The mind, they say, is not a general-purpose tool for thinking about the world, but a collection of 'modules'. The term is taken from computing where it refers to the different, specialised parts of a large program.

A classic and uncontroversial example of brain modularity is the sense of sight: specialised areas of the brain are dedicated to marshalling and manipulating the signals that come in from the retina. The faculty of sight is something distributed all the way from the eyeball to the visual cortex at the back of the brain. Though the complex and delicately

---

12 See Susan Greenfield, *The Human Brain*, which states very clearly the differences between brains and computers.

balanced mechanism of the eyeball itself is a classic example of Darwinian adaptation, it would be useless on its own. The equally complex and delicate neurological mechanisms in the brain and nerves behind it are just as necessary, and just as much the adapted products of natural selection. Sight is therefore the product of the entire visual system and as much a matter of brain architecture as of eyes and nerves.

One advantage of talking about 'senses' rather than 'modules' is that it captures the immediacy of our perceptions. The mechanisms by which we see are invisible to us. We see meaning, not information, in the world. This is true even on the very low level where popular optical illusions work.[13] The ability to interpret small images on the retina as further away than large ones, and rapidly growing images as representing something approaching, is something which is part of the normal mechanism of a growing animal brain. Above that, in separate, later-developed, but connected areas of the human brain, there are hard-wired abilities to recognise faces, and there is evidence for a considerable commonality of colour vision.

Tooby and Cosmides have found other specialised senses. Like Wilson and Daly, they are interested not in the individual, noticeable distinctions between human minds, but in the common fundamental architecture, which can be approached only indirectly. Much, perhaps most, of what we notice about our fellows is in Darwinian terms completely irrelevant even when it is innate:[14] 'most heritable psychological differences are not themselves likely to be

13 Another example of the rule that you find adaptations by looking for a bad fit with reality.

14 Another example of the way the functional genes, those responsible for an organism's development, need not map onto the analytical ones visible to selection.

complex psychological adaptations. Instead they are mostly evolutionary by-products, such as concomitants of parasite-driven selection for biochemical individuality . . . Thousands of psychological phenomena (of interest to psychopharma-cologists, neuroscientists, psychiatrists, behaviour geneticists, personality psychologists, etc.) are not adaptations, but are by-products of adaptations, negative mutations, or are the results of the neutral genetic variants.'[15]

The most important of their discoveries is a sense of fairness, or, if you prefer, a cheat-detecting module. By setting people puzzles which are logically identical but carry wholly different emotional weights, they have discovered that the emotional content of a puzzle makes a huge difference to our ability to apprehend the logic. In most contexts, logical thought comes hard to people, even university students. Using a standard method known as Wason testing, you find that fewer than a quarter of the population tested can understand the consequences of simple logical rules such as 'if P, then Q'. But when the problem is expressed in a context in which people are asked to detect cheating, rather than logical consistency, the success rate is nearly three times as great. The intellectual content is exactly the same but instead of working it out, or even understanding the problem in a way that would allow them to reproduce its underlying structure, people see the answer at once.

'People who ordinarily cannot detect violations of if–then rules can do so easily and accurately when that violation represents cheating in a situation of social exchange', they write. 'This is a situation in which one is entitled to a benefit

---

15 From an unpublished denunciation of Gould sent to the *New York Review of Books* early in 1998.

only if one has fulfilled a requirement (e.g., "If you are to eat those cookies, then you must first fix your bed"; "If a man eats cassava root, then he must have a tattoo on his chest"; or, more generally, "If you take benefit B, then you must satisfy requirement R"). Cheating is accepting the benefit specified without satisfying the condition that provision of that benefit was made contingent upon (e.g., eating the cookies without having first fixed your bed).

'When asked to look for violations of social contracts of this kind, the adaptively correct answer is immediately obvious to almost all subjects, who commonly experience a "pop out" effect. No formal training is needed. Whenever the content of a problem asks subjects to look for cheaters in a social exchange – even when the situation described is culturally unfamiliar and even bizarre – subjects experience the problem as simple to solve, and their performance jumps dramatically. In general 65–80% of subjects get it right, the highest performance ever found for a task of this kind. . . . Everywhere it has been tested (adults in the US, UK, Germany, Italy, France, Hong Kong; schoolchildren in Ecuador, Shiwiar hunter-horticulturalists in the Ecuadorian Amazon), people do not treat social exchange problems as equivalent to other kinds of reasoning problems. Their minds distinguish social exchange contents, and reason as if they were translating these situations into representational primitives such as "benefit", "cost", "obligation", "entitlement", "intentional", and "agent." Indeed, the relevant inference procedures are not activated unless the subject has represented the situation as one in which one is entitled to a benefit only if one has satisfied a requirement.'[16]

Exhaustive tests seem to have narrowed down the scope

---

16 'An Introduction to Evolutionary Psychology', on their web site.

of this cheat detection module to where it really does operate as a sense of fairness and nothing else. When the emotional content of a Wason test is fixed so that it conveys information about whether someone is bluffing (rather than cheating), or to flag a danger in a threatening situation, the answer is as hard to work out as it would be if the problem were presented in bare symbolic logic. It is even more interesting to see that the sense works to detect only cheating by reneging on bargains. Someone behaving better than they have promised is just as hard for us to see as someone not cheating at all.

Why does this matter? One answer is that it helps to explain the passions aroused by the phrase 'selfish gene'. If our brains contain a special organ to detect someone cheating, prospering unjustly at our expense, one name for the quality this organ detects is 'selfishness'. It is a word necessarily loaded with connotations of intent and hostility. They may be rubbed off it by long use among professionals. But the rubbing takes an effort which must be made afresh by everyone who takes up the concept. Often they fail to do so.

The second reason Cosmides and Tooby's research matters is that it goes right back to one of the theoretical foundations of sociobiology that George Price worked on with Maynard Smith: the applications of game theory to models of behaviour. What Tooby and Cosmides have discovered is a mechanism which might make possible the development of behaviour and instincts based on reciprocal altruism even in animals clever enough to see when it would be to their short-term advantage to cheat. 'Reciprocal altruism' was the name given by Robert Trivers to the mutually beneficial exchange of favours between unrelated animals.[17] The point about this

---

17 See Chapter 4.

form of co-operation is that it can work only if there are sanctions against cheating: the habit of giving favours will evolve only if these favours are returned. In some cases of reciprocal altruism, such as the mutually beneficial relationship between cleaner fish and their hosts, there is no forethought and, so far as we can tell, no expectation. The whole point of these models is to show how co-operative relationships can arise between animals who do not plan, scheme, or weigh the costs and benefits of their actions.

Humans do all these things. But they also co-operate. If animals like us, with foresight, are to develop reliable modes of co-operation, there must be some way of detecting cheats; for an animal which can see it is in its own interest to co-operate can also see when it is in its own interest to cheat.

From this arises the paradox set out in Blake's poem 'The Clod & the Pebble': that

> *Love seeketh not itself to please,*
> *Nor for itself hath any care,*
> *But for another gives its ease,*
> *And builds a Heaven in Hell's despair*

while it is also just as true that

> *Love seeketh only Self to please,*
> *To bind another to Its delight,*
> *Joys in another's loss of ease,*
> *And builds a Hell in Heaven's despite.*

The first of these verses describes what we think of as genuine, or human, altruism; the second, Trivers's 'reciprocal altruism'. But of course both are human, and both exist within each of us, though they are very different. Yet the sense of fairness that Tooby and Cosmides have discovered is in a curious way a link between the two. It is a mechanism by which the first of Blake's loves can arise from the second. Evolutionary psychology argues that our emotional tendencies and instincts correspond to the rules of game theory because those are the underlying realities of social relationships. So there is no contradiction between our having genuine, unselfish emotions which lead to truly unselfish actions, like those of George Price, even though we live in a world in which mutual unselfishness is in fact rewarded. So long as the 'selfish' benefits of altruistic behaviour are statistical and long-term, like all the other features that drive natural selection, individual actions and emotions can be truly selfless. In fact, they must be. The predictions of game theory are predictions about probability and long-term outcomes. If it were possible to foresee in detail the consequences of actions, and to make calculations on that basis, there would be no need of emotions (except to give us a reason for living). But such a world is impossible to imagine.

We can unite these two perspectives only in our lives, not in our intellects, and this is a point which poets have grasped more clearly and earlier than scientists or journalists playing at philosophy. 'Life, to be sure, is nothing much to lose; But young men think it is and we were young.'[18]

A Darwinian view of the wellsprings of human goodness does not make it less good; just more limited. Even George Price, who saw the limits of goodness and love in a Darwinian world, and rebelled against them with all his heart, did not by his rebellion become a saint, or even a man

---

18 A. E. Housman, 'Here Dead Lie We', in *Other Men's Flowers*, selected by Lord Wavell (Pimlico, 1997).

without aggression. You might say that he simply redistri-
buted his behaviour, so that he was ready to take infinite
pains with the powerless and miserable, and just as quick to
inconvenience the powerful people who could help him. A
man who quarrels with almost all his collaborators and does
not hesitate to get up the nose of the editor of *Nature* is not
behaving as a game theorist would expect a pure 'dove' to
behave, however much the Holy Spirit may have informed
his work among the destitute.

8

ENTER THE MEME

THE DEVELOPMENT OF evolutionary psychology from sociobiology can be understood in two ways. Looked at purely ideologically, it is a triumph for Gould and Lewontin, who have seen almost all their original objections incorporated into the project. A nice example of this comes in Tooby and Cosmides's denial (quoted on p. 140) that most of the differences between human beings are adaptive. But it came in a context of unremitting personal hostility to Gould, as we will see. E. O. Wilson's most recent book, *Consilience*, contains an account of the complexities of functional genetics so discouraging that it might have been written by Lewontin: he does not even begin on the complexities of the human genome, preferring to concentrate on the simpler and better-understood mouse, in which 'genes contributing to the texture of the hairs and skin are known from no fewer than 72 chromosome sites. At least 41 other genes have variants that cause defects in the organs of balance in the inner ear, resulting in abnormal head shaking and circling behaviour' (p. 146). This is an extraordinary retreat from the bright confidence of the original sociobiologists that everything could be reduced to the simplicities of genes and their kaleidoscopic patterns of adaptation.

Politically, however, the story seems to be one of the steady marginalisation of Gouldians and the emergence and triumph of a refined and purified sociobiology. As a new orthodoxy hardens, the Gouldians' fate is clearly to be ushered into the history books as The Men Who Were Wrong. Gould himself is particularly loathed, even though some of his criticisms of Wilson's original *Sociobiology* are now accepted even by its sympathisers.

'Parts were not even testable. Others were simply false, and, interestingly, bad Darwinian theory,' says Helena Cronin, the philosopher who runs the LSE's Darwin Seminars in London.[1] This is a startling refinement of the original position, for Cronin is the very type of what Gould calls 'Darwinian fundamentalists'. In fact, she's the only one to whom the label seems remotely fair, for she reminds me of the sort of fundamentalist I like. Both in person and as the organiser of wonderful lectures and discussions, she has been unfailingly helpful and stimulating. In writing about religion for ten years, I've grown to like a lot of fundamentalists – by no means all or even most of those I have met, but enough of them to realise that there are some people who grow best beneath a polarised light. And Helena Cronin is unnervingly like a fundamentalist cousin of mine.

Both are women of great sweetness of character, to whom the world is divided into the Elect and the Damned. What is more, for both of them the Elect are only a small class of the notionally saved. My distressing cousin distinguishes between Christianity and 'churchianity' and talks with lively pity of the poor bishops who just don't understand what it's all about. 'Everyone's a Darwinian now except for Creationists and Lamarckians,' says Helena, but you can hear the

---

1 Interview, 3 February 1998.

capital in 'Darwinian' when she talks of those who agree with her.

Both are extremely stern with those who fall from virtue. Helena told me in terms of horror of a lecturer who said that Darwinism made him feel insignificant. 'That's nothing to do with science,' she said. 'He was an ex-priest.' I asked who he might be, and she said, 'I won't tell you. I don't want to give any publicity to his views.'

Both women believe that social workers permit great evils from ignorance of the Truth. My devout cousin thinks they ignore the widespread slaughter of babies by Satanists because they don't read the Bible; Helena thinks they ignore the widespread murder of babies by stepfathers because they don't read Daly and Wilson.

Of course, there is an important difference. What my relative believes about the world is generally false, whereas what Helena believes is generally true. But I still find the similarities between them cast an interesting light on the way that scientific disputes are taking on much of the venom, as well as the importance, that theological disputes had in the days when theology was believed by educated people to deal with important features of the world. Now the emotional satisfactions of a particular religious world view can just as well be supplied by science.

Though the Dawkinsians have largely accepted their opponents' early criticisms, this has done nothing to reconcile the two camps. Cronin shrinks from the name Gould as a vampire shudders from a cross: 'I don't even like people using words like spandrels,' she says. Of course she recognises their existence. It's just that she doesn't want to give Gould any credit for recognising them. 'This serious systematic analysis of how to go about recognising that something is an adaptation – a serious systematic look at how to recognise when something is an adaptation – none of that has drawn on Gould.'[2]

Gould has about as much respect for her as she has for him. In 1992, he described her book *The Ant and the Peacock* as 'an uncritical gloss on a false and simplistic view that never was more than a caricature of Darwinian theory'.[3] This was not just nasty to her, but a gauntlet thrown down to Dawkinsians generally. Dawkins and Cronin had worked together very closely in the Eighties, though she was then a philosopher by trade (she now describes herself as 'a populariser of science'). His preface to the second edition of *The Selfish Gene* contains a fulsome tribute: 'Helena Cronin has done so much to improve on every line – every word – that she should, but for her adamant refusal, be named as joint author of all the new portions of this book' (p. xi). Maynard Smith had encouraged Cronin to publish her work; and his response to Gould was the blistering insult quoted earlier: 'A man whose ideas are too confused to be worth bothering with.'

Nothing, however, could compare to the anger of John Tooby and Leda Cosmides, the discoverers of the cheat-detection function in the brain, or sense of fairness. Their attack on Gould[4] was so blistering that the *New York Review of Books* refused to print it, so the text has so far circulated only on the Internet. 'Gould's reputation as a credible and balanced authority about evolutionary biology is non-existent among those who are in a professional position to know . . . the best way to grasp the nature of Gould's writings is to recognise them as one of the most formidable

---

2 Interview, 3 February 1998.

3 *New York Review of Books*, November 1992.

4 In response to two articles by him in the *NYRB*, 12 and 26 June 1997.

bodies of fiction to be produced in recent American letters.'

This is extraordinarily rude and unjustified. Gould is a man who has won just about every prize going for science writing. He is a professor at Harvard. He makes the case for the prosecution against evolutionary psychology; the defendants are understandably aggrieved, because he does so with all the fluency and charm that have made him loved. Whether he does enough to get the verdict he wants is questionable. Here are Tooby and Cosmides, the attorneys in their own defence, retaliating:

'The central problem is that Gould's own exposition of evolutionary biology is so radically and extravagantly at variance with both the actual consensus state of the field and the plain meaning of the primary literature that there is no easy way to communicate the magnitude of the discrepancy in a way that could be believed by those who have not experienced the evidence for themselves.'

Tooby and Cosmides's gravest charge was that Gould is deliberately ignoring the extent to which evolutionary psychology has absorbed and profited from the early criticisms of sociobiology in order to boost his own reputation at the expense of working scientists': they hate him because he is, among other things, a very good journalist. 'When the background literature is filled in, the picture of Gould inverts like a Necker cube, and his essays become revealed as mini-theatricals carefully staged for purposes of self-aggrandizement rather than for the careful and charitable pursuit of the truth. . . .

'Most of the elements of Gould's writing make no sense if they are interpreted as an honest attempt to communicate about science (e.g., why would he characterize so many researchers as saying the opposite of what they actually do?) but come sharply into focus when understood as necessary components of a world constructed for the fictional "Gould" to have heroic fantasy adventures in – adventures during which the admirable character of "Gould" can be slowly revealed . . . learned, subtle, open-minded, tolerant, funny, gracious to his opponents, a tireless adversary of cultural prejudice, able to swim upstream against popular opinion with unflinching moral courage, able to pierce the surface appearances that capture others, and indeed to be not only the most brilliant innovator in biology since Darwin, but more importantly to be the voice of humane reason against the forces of ignorance, passion, incuriosity, and injustice. The author Gould . . . is . . . none of these things.'

Some of the attacks on Gould were altogether colder. Daniel Dennett, a philosopher of artificial intelligence, rushed in with his own freshly ground axes. Dennett shares with Dawkins an agent, John Brockman, famous for his ability to command huge advances for works of popular science – Brockman offered to obtain an advance of $2m for a reporter on the *New York Times* the day after she ran a story claiming a cure for cancer had been found.[5] These advances are so large that the publishers, to earn them back, must commit themselves to thundering publicity campaigns which have done much to advance the Dawkinsian agenda.[6] The success of *The Selfish Gene* had nothing to do with Brockman, and everything to do with the vigour and excitement of its writing; but most of the subsequent books from Brockman's stable have been firmly in the Dawkinsian camp.

This is certainly true of *Darwin's Dangerous Idea*, Dennett's contribution to the Darwin wars. Dennett is a difficult

5 Gina Kolata. Her story blew up and the offer was withdrawn.
6 Steven Rose is one of the few Gouldian authors on Brockman's list.

philosopher to come to grips with. This is not because he is obscure. Though he writes that 'experience teaches there is no such thing as a thought experiment so clearly presented that no philosopher can misinterpret it', his own thought experiments are beautifully clear. He writes with tremendous vigour about important things. There is in his work a sense that we live in exciting times, when new knowledge of sorts that had previously been thought unattainable is bursting out all over. Like Dawkins, he has the quality of making the world a more interesting place than it was before you read him. The reader is buffeted, frightened and exhilarated, sometimes all at once. Yet, when the pleasure's past, a threatening doubt remains: what, exactly, has one learnt? It's like watching the Americans in Vietnam: he drenches his opponents in high explosive, declares victory, and then gets the hell out. It is difficult to think of anyone else who would have the self-confidence to write a book called simply *Consciousness Explained*, or the nerve, when it was finished, to publish the contents under that title.[7] It's a wonderful book; but it doesn't explain consciousness. The heart of Dennett's position seems to be that consciousness itself is a misleading category, and that the only way to make sense of it is to redefine all one's terms in terms of externally visible states and behaviours. Carried to extremes – the normal destination of Dennett's ideas – this leads him to assert such things as that thermostats have beliefs.[8]

---

7 I find it much easier to grasp his central ides from *Brainchildren*, a selection of shorter essays.

8 In the very limited sense that a thermostat's behaviour does rest on predictions about the outside world, or makes sense only in the light of them. In this sense, all the things we call 'beliefs' are actually states of machines, so there is no need for a 'ghost in the machine' to believe them.

One theme running through Dennett's work on evolution and artificial intelligence is the importance of engineering as a way to understand the world. What interests him is machinery and the apparent miracles it can accomplish, such as storing an entire symphony in three billion tiny holes on a compact disc. He has devoted his life to exorcising the ghost from the machine.

The objection to this programme is not that we can build a machine sufficiently complex to have free will: that seems to me an empirical question on which it is wisest to be agnostic; and even if we can't build one, it's clear that natural selection can and has done. The point is that, if you succeed, free will is what you have built: the ghost is back in the machine. It doesn't matter that this effect has been produced without God or by a Darwinian process. All working biologists agree that intelligence, curiosity, free will and so on are produced by the normal, law-bound mechanical processes of the world. The important point made by Dennett's opponents is that, once these properties have emerged, they exist. They play a part in the world which is different to that of their constituent parts. Even if you can build a bottle from which the desired genie emerges, you can't reduce the genie to the bottle once it's out.

Almost all the participants in these disputes take it for granted that the factual claims of creation and resurrection at the root of Christianity are untrue.[9] It doesn't, however, follow from this agreement that all the discoveries made by people who believed in those claims are worthless. Real

---

9 There are some knowledgeable scientists who don't. Most interesting in this context is Sam Berry, professor of genetics at University College London, who has written several books to wean evangelicals off Creationism.

human morality must be explained, not simply explained away. To say that George Price found mathematical proof of original sin is, among other things, to agree with the Christian claim that original sin exists: that there are conflicts and problems in our moral natures that have no solution.

In some moods, Dennett concedes this. There is a startling chapter in *Darwin's Dangerous Idea* full of biting, almost Gouldian criticism of sociobiology: he quotes a typically exuberant remark of E. O. Wilson's *Sociobiology* that 'our belief in morality is merely an adaptation put in place to further our reproductive ends', and comments, 'Nonsense. Our reproductive ends may have been the ends that kept us in the running until we could develop culture, and they may still play a powerful – sometimes overwhelming – role in our thinking, but that does not license any conclusion at all about our current values. . . . In a famous image, Wilson puts it this way. "The genes hold culture on a leash. The leash is very long, but inevitably values will be constrained in accordance with their effects on the human gene pool." But all this means (unless it is just false) is that, in the long run, *if* we adopt cultural practices that have disastrous effects on the human gene pool, then the human gene pool will succumb. There is no reason to think, however, that evolutionary biology shows us that our genes are powerful enough, and insightful enough to keep us from making policies quite antithetical to their interests.

'The typical inability of Wilson and other sociobiologists to see their critics as anything but religious fanatics or scientifically illiterate mysterians is yet one more sad overswing of the pendulum. [B. F.] Skinner [the founder of behaviourism] saw his critics as a bunch of Cartesian dualists and miracle-worshippers, and . . . declared:

"To man *qua* man we readily say good riddance. Only by dispossessing him can we turn to the real causes of human behaviour. Only then can we turn from the inferred to the observed, from the miraculous to the natural, from the inaccessible to the manipulable.

'Wilson and many other sociobiologists have the same bad habit of seeing anybody who disagrees with them as benighted, [and] science-fearing.'[10]

With these attitudes you would expect Dennett to come down as a firm Gouldian. But in fact he is a Dawkinsian who likes to use his own side for target practice if he can't find anyone else. His attitude to Gould is unremittingly hostile. Huge chunks of the book are devoted to startlingly mean-minded and ungenerous attacks on Gould's theories, not so much for what they are but – and Dennett is explicit about this – what they have been misunderstood to be. The man who criticises Wilson's 'inability to see his critics as anything but religious fanatics or scientifically illiterate mysterians' writes about Gould that.

He speaks not just of unpredictability but of the power of contemporary events *and personalities* to 'shape and direct the actual path' of evolution. This echoes exactly the hope that drove James Mark Baldwin to discover the effect now named for him: *somehow* we have to get personalities – consciousness, intelligence, agency – back in the driver's seat. If we can just have contingency – radical contingency – this will give the *mind* some elbow room, so it can *act*, and be *responsible* for its own destiny, instead of being the mere effect of a mindless cascade of mechanical processes. This

10 Dennett, *Darwin's Dangerous Idea*, p. 471.

conclusion, I suggest, is Gould's ultimate destination, revealed in the paths he has most recently explored.[11]

This is clearly meant as an indictment of Gould for not understanding Darwin. Why it should be so unforgivable to allow intelligence or curiosity among animals any role in evolution is not at first sight clear. No one is suggesting that animals by their own efforts can consciously direct the path of their evolution: that would be naughty Lamarckianism. But Alister Hardy, the Oxford professor of zoology who originated the aquatic ape theory, had another heresy which is interesting in this context: he thought that the behaviour of animals was important in determining the course of evolution. It is not clear how heretical this idea need be: there is one form of it which is right in the mainstream of Darwinian orthodoxy. This is the 'Baldwin effect', which allows for something that looks like, but is not, Lamarckianism. It is the process by which animals that behave in particular ways can increase the selection pressure on those genetic changes which are useful in the new way of life. As John Maynard Smith put it, 'animals and plants can adapt as individuals to changed conditions and . . . their ability to do so is of evolutionary importance. But such adaptations are not transmitted to their offspring, although changes which originate as individual adaptations may, after many generations of selection, be genetically assimilated.'[12]

Put as a general principle, this is part of the central Darwinian story about the gradual change of function which allows new organs to evolve from their precursors: only animals which try to fly will find useful mutations which

---

11 Ibid, p. 300; the italics are his.
12 Smith, *The Theory of Evolution*, p. 329.

tend to turn their cooling fins into feathers. Hence these mutations will become established only in the context of the right kind of behaviour. This much is not controversial. But Hardy went further. The importance of behaviour in setting the context in which selection acts seemed to him to establish something profound about the universe: 'No one will deny that animals living under natural conditions may come to change their behaviour; such new habits may no doubt often be due to alterations in their environment, such as failure of food supplies or the destruction of breeding sites and so on, but sometimes they may be formed through the animals themselves discovering new ways of life. They are, as I have said, inquisitive, exploratory creatures. Among the higher vertebrates a new piece of behaviour, perhaps, for example, in the gathering of food, if adopted by one or two individuals and then seen by others to be advantageous, will gradually spread by copying through the community and be passed on from parent to offspring. We see, in fact, in birds and mammals, the beginning of what might be called a tradition. In any population of animals among which there has come about a change of habit, there will turn up sooner or later individuals having small variations in structure which will make them more efficient in relation to their new behaviour; over a period of time these kinds will tend to survive rather better than those less well-equipped in this particular respect, and so the composition of the population will gradually change.

'Because the change of habit is often occasioned by changes in the environment, it is generally supposed, I think, that any selection due to such a change of habit is one differing only in degree, but not in kind, from other forms of Darwinian selection. This for me is the crux of the whole issue; I think they are radically different. I realise, of course, that it is the differential mortality in the population which brings about the survival of the more efficient type of beak in our example, and that this is obviously mediated by various factors in the environment killing off a higher proportion of the less efficient forms; nevertheless the real *initiating agent* in the process is the new behaviour-pattern, the *new habit*. Although new habits may, as I have said, frequently result from environmental changes, they are by no means always so formed; among vertebrates it must often be the restless, exploring and perceptive animals that discover new ways of living, new sources of food. This searching, inquisitive type of behaviour has no doubt been fostered and developed by selection just because it pays dividends.'[13]

Hardy went on to develop these arguments in an explicitly religious direction: in that form they collide still more violently with Dawkinsian orthodoxy. But even this limited role for the mind is anathema to Dennett. He believes that all mental and cultural life can itself be reduced to a mindless Darwinian process, conducted by things called memes. The name,[14] and part of the idea, comes from Richard Dawkins, who wrote:

I think that a new kind of replicator has recently emerged on this very planet. It is staring us in the face. It is still in its infancy, still drifting clumsily about in its primeval soup, but already it is achieving evolutionary change at a rate that leaves the old gene panting far behind. . . .

---

13 Hardy, *Darwin and the Spirit of Man*, p. 145.

14 Lots of people who now use the term don't mean quite what Dawkins meant; there has also been considerable hybridisation with the ideas of conjecture and refutation descended from Karl Popper, which have migrated out of philosophy to regions where the predators are less efficient.

Examples of memes are tunes, ideas, catch-phrases, clothes fashions, ways of making pots or of building arches. Just as genes propagate themselves in the gene pool by leaping from body to body via sperms or eggs, so memes propagate themselves in the meme pool by leaping from brain to brain via a process which, in the broad sense, can be called imitation. If a scientist hears, or reads about, a good idea, he passes it on to his colleagues and students. He mentions it in his articles and his lectures. If the idea catches on, it can be said to propagate itself, spreading from brain to brain.[15]

The argument for the existence of memes comes from syllogism rather than observation, though when you first grasp it you see memes everywhere. The syllogism goes something like this: if Darwinian algorithm is the only way we know to generate order and complexity in nature, which it is, and if our minds are full of order and complexity, which they are, then there must be a Darwinian algorithm operating on something inside them, and that something we shall call memes.

Dawkins has since retreated from actually advocating this position as true, while Dennett has taken it much further. *Darwin's Dangerous Idea* asks the question 'Could there be a science of memetics?' but nowhere spoils the argument by answering it.

The good reason for this bashfulness is that memes are enormous fun: they can explain anything at all. A sparkling example of this flexibility was provided by the science writer Oliver Morton, who replied to the question 'Why do I keep meeting clever sexy women who believe in memes and make me feel a plodding old pedant because I don't?' with

15 *The Selfish Gene*, p. 192.

the following memetic breakthrough: 'Because memes have found that sexy women spread them well, and have found that the adaptation (intellectual vigour) needed to conquer a marginal niche (plodding old pedants) is an unreasonable use of their resources. Memes adapted to plodding old pedants become so complex and epicyclic that they cannot be passed on, and thus die out.'[16]

I think that makes Morton the founder of selfish meme theory. But, as the example of early sociobiology shows, this kind of exuberance of explanation is normally a sign that a theory can't actually predict anything. So there is a bad reason for failing to answer the question 'Could there be a science of memetics?'

The difficulties are more honestly faced by Dawkins, who lists important objections. They mostly boil down to one: that memes are not very like genes at all when you come to examine them. Almost everything suggested as a meme-candidate is much more like a phenotype, or interactor, than a gene, or a replicator. Just as importantly, there seems to be no logical way for memes to be connected to each other in the way that genetic characters are. Genes occupy particular places or loci on chromosomes. If a gene spreads through a population of animals, it is at the expense of a variant form which might be doing the same job less well. This process of clearly defined replacement is what enables natural selection to produce the effect of design. But it is a very rare idea which can be said to replace another entirely and exactly, in the way that analytical genes can do within populations. Ideas, or memes, fit together much more like animals, in a complex ecology, than they do like genes competing for slots on a chromosome.

---

16 Personal communication.

These differences matter, but perhaps not enough to finish off the idea. Even if ideas are much more like animals, or even plants, than genes – being complex, unpredictable, and capable of finding their own nourishment – once you have started thinking of them as biological, it is difficult to go back to considering them as expressions of eternal verities. In fact it is extraordinarily hard to rid yourself of the idea that memes may exist, once you have come across it. And for anyone committed to the idea that Darwinian processes are the fundamental explanation for everything interesting, memes provide a very necessary way to assert that minds and ideas are not determined by genetic puppeteers. Despite this bad reason for believing in them, memes, like gods, have merits even if they lack existence. For one thing, they force attention onto the collective nature of ideas. In an age when everyone is encouraged to think themself original and not merely unique, it is a useful corrective to see our inner lives as essentially social. The psychologist Susan Blackmore (who is a believer) likes them partly because they tell her students that they don't own or originate their own ideas.

One does not have to believe in memes to agree that ideas are shared things, like language, and that we are much less in control of what we think than we would like to be. The enormous difficulty that all traditions of meditation or contemplative prayer have found when their followers try to empty their minds is one powerful argument for this. None the less, one of the most widely shared ideas in the Western world at the moment is that people are individuals sufficiently autonomous to be able to choose freely what they believe. This is nearly as ridiculous as the 'blank slate' theory of human personality; and Darwinian arguments are just as effective against it. But that does not make them true.

Ideas, and culture more generally, can perfectly well be shared, autonomous, and to a large degree independent of the wishes and personality of individual bearers, without being made out of things that work like genes. Money is also a social artefact, and economies behave in complex ways that are to a large degree independent of the wishes of their bearers. That does not mean there is a Nobel prize waiting for the man who explains it in terms of 'selfish dollars'.

There might, however, be fame and wealth available for anyone who could come up with a truly scientific theory of human personality. Another reason for Susan Blackmore's delight in memes is that they seem to offer a chance to sweep away the whole mess of present psychological theories. When people can't agree what mind is, what it does, or what they are studying, then a radical behaviourism of the sort proposed by Dennett – in which you study, without, so far as is possible, any preconceptions, what the world presents – may be a way out of a lot of blind alleys. There is a sense in which meme theory is the culmination of a long project to get the demons out of the world. First Descartes separated matter and spirit: then the laws governing the movement of matter were discovered. Then the divisions between living and dead matter went, so that life, instead of requiring some separate essence, turned out to be just matter arranged in a particular way. Finally, the memeticists hope to remove the animating personality from human beings, or at least to expose it as an illusion: they think that our belief in other people's personalities, and *a fortiori* in our own, will turn out to be as superstitious as the belief that the woods are haunted by leprechauns. For Blackmore, the belief that other people have selves, and so that we do too, has no more scientific worth than a politician's cv: both are vivid, inaccurate précis constructed for social advancement.

One of the most interesting shots at thinking of culture biologically comes from the anthropologist Dan Sperber, who talks about an 'epidemiology of ideas'. This sounds as if it is a comparison with 'viruses of the mind' but it is more subtle, or at least without the overtones of teenage science fiction. For what interests Sperber is the qualities that make ideas copiable. As he points out, the characteristic fate of an idea is to be changed every time it is transmitted, whereas the defining character of a gene is that it is stable.

'Whatever their differences and their merits, past approaches share a crucial defect: they take the basic process of cultural transmission to be one of replication, and consider alterations in transmissions as accidents . . . [but] what human communication achieves in general is merely some degree of resemblance between the communicator's and the audience's thoughts. Strict replication, if it exists at all, should be viewed as just a limiting case of maximal resemblance, rather than as the norm of communication.'[17]

But the ways we change stories as we pass them on may take regular and predictable forms, he argues. There are some patterns of information that we find easier to pass on than others. What is more, different sorts of ideas are copied in different ways, according to different rules. In other words, the important factor in the transmission of ideas is what they can do for people, not what people can do for them. This seems so modest and obvious a point that it is hard to understand how radical it is in the memetic context. In fact, Sperber's originality only really appears in the light of the Dawkinsians' extraordinary hostility towards religion, which deserves and will get a chapter to itself. It is possible to develop even this limited idea of cultural epidemiology in

---

17 Sperber, *Explaining Culture*, pp. 82–3.

interesting ways. Asking what ways there are for information to be transmitted seems to be moving towards all sorts of strange theories about the deep structure of the brain – E. O. Wilson's list of epigenetic rules in *Consilience* bears a marked resemblance to Jung's ideas of a collective unconscious. But Sperber is not so ambitious at first sight.

This may be because he has a clear grasp of the size of the task awaiting him. Like Dennett and Blackmore (and the early Marxists) he wants a radical materialism, in which there are no metaphysical entities at all. 'We understand reasonably well how material things fit into the world; but we don't know that there are immaterial things and, if there are, we don't know how they fit. Hence, for any class of entities – rocks, memories, or cultural representations – a materialist account, if it is available at all, is preferable on grounds of intelligibility and parsimony.'[18] The materialist account of meaning is, then, that a meaning is certain patterns of brain activation reliably and causally connected to certain exterior and observable events. Alternately, a meaning (or belief) is certain patterns of activation in a computer which are reliably and causally connected to the outside world.

The connection between external affairs and brain states, though, is neither simple nor obvious. There is something going on in my brain to represent the fact I am sitting and typing this. But that is too vague, general, and implicit a form of knowledge to show up on a brain scan. Existing scanners would show the activation of particular areas of my brain as the words of the I am writing sentence pass through my mind.

But what would the scanner show *om jag säger samma sak på Svenska* (if I say the same thing in Swedish)? The meaning

18 Ibid, p. 80.

has not changed, but the brain circuitry used has. The Holy Grail of the materialist, Dawkinsian program is not just a better and more detailed scanner, which would describe what every neurone was doing, but the understanding necessary to interpret such a picture: teasing out a reliable pattern of connections between brain structure and meaning, so that you could, with a sufficiently detailed scanner, read the contents of my mind off a computer screen. There is an awful lot more confidence in the feasibility of this project among philosophers than among neurologists.

9

AND THE MEME RATHS OUTGRABE

WHEN A NORMALLY educated secular person first deals with religious belief, it can appear a kind of insanity. I have spent ten years writing about religion as a journalist and I am still shocked by some things that the devout believe. There is a Rastafarian legend that when the Prime Minister of Jamaica said something cutting about the Emperor Haile Selassie's lapdogs, one of the chihuahuas in question roared at him like a lion. Among Charismatic Roman Catholics it is an article of faith that eighty thousand pilgrims saw the sun doing acrobatics in the sky when the Virgin Mary appeared to three shepherd girls at Fátima in Portugal in 1916; and they tend to miss the point if you reply to them that this proves only that eighty thousand eye witnesses can be wrong. And so on.

The first time I interviewed the Chief Rabbi, Dr Jonathan Sacks, a man with a double first (one of those degrees being in philosophy) from Cambridge, he defended to me the proposition that Moses himself wrote or dictated all five books of the Pentateuch, including those passages in which his own death is described. That is the most shocking thing I have ever heard an intellectual say – at least, the most shocking *trahison des clercs*. I may think that religious belief is ineradicable and useful; I don't think it is any guarantee of truth.

It is also true that religions are dangerous. They shape some of the worst expressions of our nature. I have seen young Croat soldiers playing with live hand grenades outside a church, as if they were protected by the icons of the Virgin Mary, Queen of Peace, pasted on the butts of their Kalashnikovs. A sociobiologist would hold that the capacity to take pleasure in the death and suffering of others is innate and adaptive in the human species: it was there before religion; the same could be said of the division that humans so naturally make of the world into tribes, in-groups and out-groups. But almost every expression of these tendencies recorded in history has had a religious element. It's difficult to think of any lasting or atrocious conflict in which religion has not been one of the factors separating and defining the two sides. At first sight it looks as if the war between Nazi Germany and Communist Russia, two officially atheist states, would qualify. But in fact religion was used by both sides alongside their officially atheist ideologies: almost the first thing that Stalin did when Russia was invaded was to release from the camps any priests who were still alive, and allow them to celebrate the Orthodox liturgy once more. Hitler, too, was careful to ensure that he had a majority of the Church backing him.

Yet given that religions are always powerful and some-times extremely dangerous, and that religious belief can make sane men assert lunacies, it still does not follow that religions are the product of evil spirits, or selfish memes.

Religions are the oldest and the strongest cultural systems we know of. The history of gene–culture co-evolution must in fact have been to a large extent the story of gene–religion co-evolution. If there is any adaptive function to human culture, religions must themselves be adaptive. Reliable studies show that religious faith is, in fact, a pretty good predictor of psychic and physical health. What's interesting is that it hardly matters what this faith is: an approach which is carried to extremes by Alcoholics Anonymous. Sometimes I think that AA is the most interesting religious development of the century. All it demands is faith in a Higher Power: you are not required to discuss what it is, or even whether it exists. Yet this vague, inarticulate self-contradictory psychic judo works. It is an essential part of the network of social support which enables alcoholics to construct a self which doesn't have to drink.

So even if truth is not a sufficient condition for a religion to arise or triumph, it may yet be a necessary one. It is unlikely that any belief, or complex of beliefs, would widely or for long be held by anyone if it did not correspond in important respects to the real world. A statement which asserts a historical falsehood may none the less encode an emotional truth. This is a remark that gets us onto difficult ground. I do not mean to suggest that wishing something were true can make it so. Elvis stays dead no matter how much his followers wish otherwise. No doubt the same is true of Jesus. But it's a great mistake to take these facts personally, as if the universe meant them as a lesson to us. And if we must take the universe personally, it is probably wiser and saner to believe and hope in resurrections than to rush around like the Scotsman in *Dad's Army*, crying, 'We're all doomed!'

Mary Midgley put this point vividly in *Evolution as a Religion*, when she wrote: 'Possibly, for human beings, the only alternative to thinking of the universe as, in some vast and remote way, purposive and benign, is to think of it as purposive and radically malignant. It may simply not be within our capacity – except of course by just avoiding thought – to think of it as having no sort of purpose or direction whatever. And since the notion that it is radically malignant is a crazy one, benignity seems to be the only usable option.'

She went on to make a point just as important: that our view of the universe is not characterised by God-like detachment and can't be. Like the Christian God, people who think themselves above the universe constantly find themselves dragged back in to take sides in the struggles between hope and despair; and it matters which side we take.

'People who firmly deny this benignity are extremely easily led on to assert that something actually vicious is present instead. They very readily begin to talk like A. E. Housman about "Whatever brute and blackguard made the world", or say like [Thomas] Hardy that "the President of the Immortals . . . had ended his sport with Tess".[1] Obviously this kind of talk has its passing value as a corrective to a complacent or childish kind of religion. But if it is taken seriously as more than a passing corrective, it seems at once to become no less superstitious than what it was trying to correct, and also far less usable for life.

'Such visions cannot be inert. They exist to guide conduct; it is of their nature to influence life. But the only practical consequences which this one seems capable of producing are abominable. It imposes either a fatalistic, paralysing resignation to human helplessness before destruc-

---

1 Housman, *Last Poems* (1922), no. 9; Hardy, *Tess of the d'Urbervilles* (London: Penguin, 1978), p. 489.

tive forces, or a positive justification for joining them in selfish mayhem.'[2]

People who recognise this are put in a difficult position. It is very likely that the explicit doctrines of any religion are false. But these falsehoods will contain, or imply, important truths,[3] sometimes about subjects which have nothing to do with the ostensible content of an idea or a pattern of behaviour. This is the reasoning behind Marvin Harris's account of cultures, but it can be generalised to all sorts of beliefs. So it is worth applying this kind of reasoning to a belief in memes, for there is no doubt that this, too, can lead to stupidities and towards cruelties. In fact, a great deal of the silliness surrounding the idea of memes is very closely tied to religion. Dawkins, Daniel Dennett, and their friend the psychologist and militant atheist Nicholas Humphrey talk about the 'memes' they disapprove of in exactly the same way that fundamentalists talk about 'demons'. In both cases, their opponents' ideas are dismissed as the result, quite literally, of possession. If this is your point of entry into their ideas it makes it hard to take seriously anything else they have to say, which is unfortunate.

'When you plant a fertile meme in my mind you literally parasitize my brain, turning it into a vehicle for the meme's propagation in just the way that a virus may parasitize the genetic mechanism of a host cell', Humphrey wrote to Dawkins – and of course the example he used of this sinister process was religious: 'And this isn't just a way of talking – the meme for, say, "belief in life after death" is actually realised physically, millions of times over, as a structure in

---

2 Mary Midgley, *Evolution as a Religion*, p. 136.
3 The clearest and most delightful example of how to think about religious belief is still William James's *The Varieties of Religious Experience*.

the nervous systems of individual men the world over.'[4]

The use of 'parasitise' here runs into immediate difficulties. One is that there is no easy answer to the question 'what is being parasitised?' It can't be brains, unless you are prepared to say that plants 'parasitise' the earth. Dennett gets round this by talking instead about memes 'infesting' brains, which preserves the strangeness of the idea, and the delicious tinge of horror, without being specific about the relationship between ideas and brains. But of course the real point of 'parasite' language is that it enables its users to be nasty about ideas they disapprove of. In theory, Humphrey's and Dawkins's ideas about memes are just as much parasites as are the ideas they oppose. In practice, they use this abusive language only to characterise ideas they disapprove of. They spread their memes: their religious opponents are infected by 'viruses of the mind'.

This is held to justify any amount of persecution. After all, what is being persecuted is not human, but some kind of virus. One culmination of the process was reached in 1997, when Nick Humphrey argued that parents should be forbidden by the state to transmit beliefs he finds obnoxious. 'Children have a right not to have their minds addled by nonsense. And we as a society have a duty to protect them from it. So we should no more allow parents to teach their children to believe in the literal truth of the Bible, or that the planets rule their lives, than we should allow parents to knock their children's teeth out or lock them in a dungeon.'[5]

What makes this suggestion truly extraordinary is that it was delivered as a contribution to human rights, as part of an

---

4 Quoted in *The Selfish Gene*, p. 192.
5 'What shall we Tell the Children?', Amnesty Lecture, Oxford, 21 February 1997.

Amnesty lecture, and the programme of censorship he was advocating was justified on the grounds that teaching children falsehoods is a wrong as great as mutilating them physically. Something has gone very badly wrong when the pieties of atheism are so stifling that no one notices anything odd in the proposal to take into care children who are allowed to read an astrology column (or perhaps merely to jail or fine their parents) simply because this modest proposal is justified by appeals to scientific knowledge and human rights.

If nothing else, this shows that the attitudes which made the Inquisition obnoxious are able to survive and flourish in an atmosphere untainted by Christian orthodoxy and that the problematic consequences of religion cannot be abolished merely by abolishing religious belief. Humphrey is able, in the course of one and the same lecture, to argue that religious belief or superstition must necessarily crumble into dust at the touch of science, and that it is such a cruel and irreversible mutilation of a child's mind to teach that the Bible is literally true that it must be banned by law.

And these are the people who disparage theology as intellectual tennis played without a net.

How else are we to describe their kind of atheism? Perhaps as a sort of intellectual fox-hunting: a socially reassuring canter across agreeable countryside, in pursuit of a quarry that cannot bite back.

Dawkins is known among the literate public in England at least as much as an opponent of religion as a supporter of evolution – partly, of course, because Creationists are a tiny and bewildered remnant in this country, so that to be interested in them is a greater distinction than to be a biologist, however distinguished. The general newspaper-reading public may not fully understand the details of the theory of evolution any more than they know the diameter of the earth, but they certainly accept it, just as they believe the earth is round. If anyone is a reviled minority in this country it is not Darwinians, but devout fundamentalist Christians.

I have occasionally attended Creationist conferences and public meetings, and never found more than two hundred people at the most. Evolution is just not an issue in this country, except among the most head-banging Christian groupuscules, and even there it tends to drift in from America. The only remotely famous Christian in this country who is a Creationist is Ian Paisley, who gained his doctorate, and much of his style, from a fundamentalist college in the American Bible Belt.

Around the world, Creationist Protestantism is a minority form of Christianity. The largest single Christian denomination in the world, which also has the merit for this argument of taking its own pronouncements reasonably seriously, is the Roman Catholic Church, which fully accepts the Darwinian doctrine of natural selection as true and has rejected the idea that the book of Genesis is historical ever since Augustine, in the fifth century.

In America there is of course serious[6] and well-organised opposition to Darwinism, just as there is a serious and well-organised movement to ensure that teenage children have ready access to automatic weapons and ammunition, and a large body of opinion that holds that all useful science originated in Africa. The sanity or historical plausibility of a message has no necessary correlation with its political importance in American culture. Despite a succession of crushing court victories which have kept 'Creation Science'

---

6 Though not intellectually.

out of publicly funded classrooms, there is a steady quiet pressure which has kept explicit Darwinism out of widely sold textbooks, too.[7] Not all of this can be put down to the malign influence of American Protestantism. As much, it seems to me, comes from the profoundly democratic and capitalist nature of America, which holds that everyone has a right to believe what pleases them, especially if there is money to be made out of this belief. The love of truth is the weakest of all human passions, said A. E. Housman, and it does not do much for the popularity of evolutionary biology to point out that it is true. The real enemy of science is not organised religion, but the guerrilla forces of disorganised credulity.

One of the reasons why discussing religions as 'viruses of the mind' is so stupid is that it does not ask the question why certain beliefs are preferred to others: what they do for their bearers – or, when it does, it answers this question in terms so crass as to be worthless.

Take, for example, a religion which almost every reader of this book would agree is founded on lies. Mormonism,[8] so far as any historian can tell, was invented in 1827 by Joseph Smith, a gifted, attractive and unscrupulous young man who had earlier tried his luck as a treasure hunter. The founding scriptures, which he produced in seventy-five days in a sort of trance, pretending to have received them on golden tablets from an angel, were a rambling parody of the King James version of the Bible. After his wife caught him with a servant girl, there was considerable tension in the household, resolved only when God told him to institute

---

7 See Dorothy Nelkin, 'The Science-Textbook Controversies'.
8 A scrupulous, witty and thoughtful guide is Malise Ruthven's book *The Divine Supermarket*.

polygamy, explaining: 'If any man espouse a virgin, and desire to espouse another, and the first give her consent, and if he espouse the second, and they are virgins, and have vowed to no other man, then he is justified; he cannot commit adultery for they are given unto him; for he cannot commit adultery with what belongeth unto him and to no one else.'[9]

This proprietorial disposition of virgins was not the only feature of God's revelation which caused trouble with the outside world. God also explained to Smith that blacks were irredeemably inferior and could never be admitted to the priesthood, a doctrine He did not tell the Mormon elders to modify until 1974, when His people were threatened with civil-rights lawsuits.

An early, disillusioned associate said of Smith and his chief helper: 'They lie by revelation, swindle by revelation, cheat and defraud by revelation, run away by revelation, and if they do not mend their ways, I fear they will at last be damned by revelation.'[10] Leaving a trail of brethren similarly blind to his charismatic qualities behind him, Smith and his followers moved steadily westwards, until they founded a community at Nauvoo on the banks of the Mississippi river.

In 1844, Smith was murdered by a lynch mob in a neighbouring town. Eighteen months later, his successor as leader of the Church, Brigham Young, led the surviving community (at the time of the Great Trek, most members were recent immigrants) on a westward march of scarcely credible heroism and endurance until they fetched up in Utah. There, they and their descendants flourished, until there are

---

9 This justification was not in the original *Book of Mormon*; Smith had a later, and opportune, 'revelation'.

10 Quoted in Malise Ruthven, *The Divine Supermarket*, p. 73.

now some 6 million Mormons around the world; their Church is immensely rich, and the prospects for it look as bright as those for any other religion.

Clearly, Mormonism has been extremely good to its adherents. If the real purpose and justification of cultures is to spread the genes of their holders, it is hard to see how any sociobiologist could possibly resist conversion to Mormonism.[11] Instead of serial monogamy, one could have four wives in parallel, with a corresponding increase in the throughput of genetic material.

It is not just polygamy which makes Mormonism a good vehicle of gene transmission. The value of religions as ways to generate social cohesion is admitted by most Darwinians. There is also the discipline and sense of common purpose with which the pioneers were endowed on their epic trek to Salt Lake City, and the consequent high morale, which must have helped to keep many of them alive. And if the social nature of human beings did evolve to suit small bands of hunter-gatherers surrounded by potentially hostile tribes, the Mormons were thrown by their religion into an environment to which they were perfectly psychologically adapted. Even the argument about polygamy is more subtle than it can appear: it's not just an arrangement to allow men to get laid as often as possible. Publicly sanctioned polygamy also ensures women economic support for the children they bear (though the present-day remnant of polygamous

---

11 This hypothesis could, I think, be tested. Because the Mormons believe that their ancestors can be drawn into their own covenant with God, they have become tremendous genealogists. So you could look at their records of the original converts to discover whether they had had more descendants than their Christian relatives. I think you would find that conversion to Mormonism was a tremendous indicator of reproductive success.

Mormons are notorious for putting their spare wives and children on welfare). It may be for most women less ideal than monogamy but in pre-industrial societies it is better than widowhood or single motherhood. Given the enormously important role that religious explanations play in the ways that almost all cultures explain themselves, it is hard to have any kind of adaptive explanation for human culture that does not embrace religion.

There is a further and deeper sense in which religion seems to be adaptive or to cause human flourishing. This lies in its effects on the individual, which are rather different from its effects as a social glue. The two may conflict and often have. The figure of the prophet burning with his own righteousness is a familiar one, but he may end up burning in the marketplace for the edification of his former followers. That is an extreme case of the conflict; usually it is successfully avoided: the Roman Catholic Church has devoted huge and usually successful efforts to containing personal religious experience within a public structure.[12] The religious organisation of societies has often helped them to survive and to cohere. This much is admitted by most atheists. But there is the rather different matter of whether the exercise of the religious imagination is good for individuals.

It is difficult to find a term for this quality that is not loaded. I would like to use 'spirituality' but it comes with all sorts of unattractive baggage and I want a word to suggest a faculty which even atheists may see the need for. It is the ability to draw strength from a feeling of awe and delight in

---

12 The Catholic Church is distinguished in this context not by its intolerance of heretics but by its degree of organisation, which makes heresy possible.

the world, and of our own insignificance before what awes and delights us. This can find numerous incompatible expressions: in that, the religious imagination is like the language instinct. If it is developed to the point where it is useful, it automatically excludes some people in whom the development has taken incompatible paths. The search for a fundamental religion, or perennial philosophy, may be an example of the same sort of mistake as looking for the 'natural' language that children would speak if uncorrupted.

The exercise of the religious imagination is always socially conditioned, and often in surprising ways. When Alister Hardy, towards the end of his life, began a project to collect and classify religious experiences as if they were any other subject for scientific enquiry, he found, first, that they were extremely common; and, second, that their expression varied according to the social class and degree of education of the experiencer. If you are poor you see ghosts and demons: if you are better educated, you see spirits or experience pure love.

To dismiss this as temporal lobe stimulation is to make a category mistake, unless you are prepared to dismiss your own experience reading this as cortical stimulation.[13] Both our sense of self and also the stories we tell about the world presumably consist in patterns of activation in the brain. But we have no idea how to map them neurologically. Talking in the language of philosophy, or even of novelists, is for the moment a more precise and informative description of what is going on than using brain language figuratively.

So 'the religious imagination' is obviously something that goes on in the brain. It may or may not reflect some features

---

13 It may not be intellectual stimulation. That is another matter, for which I apologise.

of external reality. What suggests that it does is that exercising the religious imagination is good for people. In all the surveys that I know, religious belief is an indicator of physical and mental health. Praying for other people doesn't help them, as was most famously and elegantly demonstrated by Francis Galton in the nineteenth century when he studied the death rate among the royal families of Europe, whose health was prayed for in every church on the continent every Sunday. But it seems to help the person praying.

As an atheist myself, I find this fact depressing. And it is certainly extremely odd that all these prayers to all these different gods seem to work as well as each other. But it does seem to be the case that there is a general human appetite for transcendence, or spiritual refreshment, though people vary in it as they do in other appetites. Among biologists, it seems to take expression in a hunger for wilderness. It is the quality that makes 'naturalist' such a term of praise among them. This is clearest in E. O. Wilson, whose autobiography describes a terrible tension between the ineffable and utterly necessary experiences he has had in the wild and the inadequacy of Christianity to explain or reflect them. But there is a similar note of overwhelming romantic necessary longing in Hamilton's descriptions of his researches in Brazil.

It's clear that these experiences have shaped their lives as much as have their intellectual ones. And if their personalities are built by their genes as much as they themselves believe, the capacity to feel and to sate such spiritual hungers must have been preserved, if not enhanced, by natural selection.

I think it is the need to avoid conclusions of this sort which leads memeticists like Dawkins to argue that memes are dangerous, autonomous, and concerned only with their own good, not with that of their bearers. Otherwise they would have to develop a more sophisticated theory of truth, and that would be no fun at all. There is another possible, and more creditable, explanation: that they see the need to keep distinct two selective systems, acting on different entities, ideas and bodies. Both explanations may in fact apply.

The sudden, wrenching transition between genetic determinism for animals and memetic determinism for humans which is found in *The Selfish Gene* seems to stem, partly at least, from the need to avoid admitting that many of the things that humans believe (including religions and meme theory) can be preserved because they satisfy emotional and even practical needs. It corresponds to a sharp and surely unrealistic division between emotion and idea, or rationalism and superstition.

There is a division of view here, between E. O. Wilson, on the one hand, and Dawkins, Dennett and Humphrey on the other. Wilson underwent a classic evangelical conversion as an adolescent. He has since rejected it, and in the early Eighties, Ullica Segerstråle, a sociologist of science who studied Wilson's feud with Lewontin, came to the conclusion that a large part of their differences stemmed from Wilson's zeal to replace religion with science.[14] But he does see religion as important and adaptive. Religious codes seem to him to contain vital cultural information, which must be good for genes. It's not clear from his latest works whether he still believes that science can entirely replace religion, though he still writes as if this were the ultimate aim.

Dawkins and Humphrey, on the other hand, write as if science had already replaced religion: it's just that we are too stupid to understand this. 'Conversions from superstition to

14 See her article 'Colleagues in Conflict'.

science have been and are everyday events. They have probably been part of our personal experience. Those who have been walking in darkness have seen a great light,' said Humphrey in his Amnesty lecture. (Note, incidentally, the use of a religious metaphor to drive home an atheist point, a trope they find irresistible.) 'By contrast conversions from science back to superstition are virtually unknown. It just does not happen that someone who has learnt and understood science and its methods and who is then offered a non-scientific alternative chooses to abandon science.'

But of course these conversions happen all the time. Every measure of popular belief over the last fifty years shows that unscience is growing in popularity by leaps and bounds. Astrology, ufology, and every imaginable form of New Age crap grow steadily more popular. So, too, does the number of organised Creationists in the US. The Internet, which is accessible only to people of a reasonable degree of education, pullulates with superstition. There is a strong and recognisable strain of scientifically educated fundamentalists in all religions. It looks as if a technical education predisposes people to take scriptures as literally as if they were instruction manuals. Scientifically educated fundamentalists may well suffer from intellectual dishonesty amounting to a sort of cognitive dissonance. But is their condition any worse than the one that Humphrey has talked himself into?

His problems cannot be attributed to stupidity. He is a very clever man. And yet a moment's examination of the world shows that what he claims about the relative rationality of science and religion isn't true and couldn't be true: 'Science doesn't cajole; it doesn't dictate; it lays out the factual and theoretical arguments as to why something is so – and invites us to assent to them, and to see it for ourselves, Hence, by the time someone has understood a scientific explanation they have in an important sense already chosen it as theirs. How different is the case of religious or superstitious explanation. Religion makes no pretence of engaging its devotees in any process of rational discovery or choice. If we dare ask *why* we should believe something, the answer will be because it has been written in the Book, because this is our tradition, because it was good enough for Moses, because you'll go to heaven that way. Or, as often as not, don't ask.'[15]

This is ludicrous. All religions pretend to rationality, and most of them attain it. They are constantly giving believers reasons to believe, and these reasons are constantly being rationally confirmed. What on earth does Humphrey suppose goes on in Catholic universities, Orthodox Jewish seminaries, or even in the Islamic academies at Q'om, if not rational argument? It may be based on premises he finds repugnant or false, but it is conducted with a high degree of sophistication and respect for the facts. It is precisely the long attempt to construct rationally defensible, coherent, and yet still flexible systems of thought which makes these religions so hard to change. The intellectual system of any given religion turns as slowly as a supertanker because, like a supertanker's, its parts are closely and necessarily linked, which gives it tremendous size and momentum.

To take a particularly controversial example: the Roman Catholic ban on artificial contraception, which can appear the summit of irrationality, is there because the Church has argued itself into a corner. It is not a gratuitous act of perverse stupidity. It is a closely reasoned one. And the authority that enforces it is called the *magisterium* – a word which derives from *magister*, meaning teacher. It is the

---

15 'What shall we Tell the Children?'

intention of Pope John Paul II that Catholics (and others) should be persuaded by his arguments – not because they are his, but because they are excellent and subtle. And when he issues an encyclical banning discussion, this is at least partly because – as a former philosopher – he thinks the argument is over. It has been decided on rational grounds. Anyone who disagrees is blinded by self-interest or stupidity. There is nothing uniquely authoritarian or hostile to intellectual enquiry in this. He's wrong, of course, but that's another matter. When the same Pope proclaims that Darwinism is established as a truth which needs no further discussion, I don't hear Dawkins, Humphrey, or anyone else complaining that this is a vile abuse of the gullibility of a billion Catholics. Yet it is as much an act of teaching and of judgement as his pronouncements on contraception.

Nor is it the case that scientific truth is in practice accessible to everyone. Some people are too stupid to grasp them (just as the Pope would argue that some people are too wicked or too proud to grasp important moral truths). Even for those who might in principle understand what is going on, life's too short to do the experiments. It is too short even to understand why the experiments need doing. The general theory of evolution is probably about as complex as science can get and still be graspable by the unaided intellect. Most of the detailed work at the root of the controversies in this book simply has to be taken on faith by the general reader, or even the non-specialist scientist. When George Price, a trained chemist and experienced computer programmer, set out to check Hamilton's work on kin selection it took a year and drove him mad. There were no experiments involved in this, either: it was a matter of checking and understanding the mathematical reasoning. The mathematical hindrances to understanding science are large enough to exclude many people, perhaps most of them, from any informed discussion.

Nor is mathematics the only barrier to understanding. Lewontin has argued that 'even individual scientists are ignorant about most of the body of scientific knowledge, and it is not simply that biologists do not understand quantum mechanics. If I were to ask my colleagues in the Museum of Comparative Zoology at Harvard to explain the evolutionary importance of RNA editing in trypanosomes, they would be just as mystified by the question as the typical well-educated reader.

'Science is urged on us as a model of rational deduction from publicly verifiable facts, freed from the tyranny of unreasoning authority. . . . [But] given the immense extent, inherent complexity, and counterintuitive nature of scientific knowledge, it is impossible for anyone, including non-specialist scientists, to retrace the intellectual paths that lead to scientific conclusions about nature. In the end we must trust the experts and they, in turn, exploit their authority as experts and their rhetorical skills to secure our attention and our belief in things that we do not really understand.'[16]

The point of this argument is not that science and religion are equally valid alternatives, between which one is free to choose. The point is that both exist in a social matrix. Both depend for their transmission on moral qualities, like scrupulousness, and truth-telling, and neither can appeal to an unmediated outside authority, whether this is God or Experiment.

Both Gouldians and Dawkinsians reject creationism, of course; and both are convinced Darwinians; but their

---

16 *New York Review of Books*, 9 January 1997.

attitudes to Creationists differ profoundly, and are one of the most reliable touchstones for distinguishing the movements.

Gould, who appeared as a witness for the scientists in the last great Creationist trial in Alabama in 1982, has none the less written sympathetically about the reasons which have led Americans to reject Darwinism. Lewontin has described with wry amusement an early debate with Creationists, in which he partnered Carl Sagan; but he now believes that this was not really an argument about science at all but one about the distribution of power in society and the relative prestige of different elites. You will search in vain for such sympathy among the Dawkinsians. The raucous, jeering hostility with which they treat religion is extraordinary. Nicholas Humphrey, in his book *Soul Searching*, discusses Jesus as a conjuror. Dawkins writes of the contorted faces of flatfish (evidence that they have evolved from ancestors which swam upright), '[This] is a good . . . [argument] to thrust down the throats of religious fundamentalists'.[17]

The jeering in this goes beyond attacking particular beliefs. Dawkins argues that any religious belief is irrational. Perhaps 'argument' is overstating his position, since he skips over such difficulties with a simple definition: 'But what, after all, is faith? It is a state of mind that leads people to believe something – it doesn't matter what – in the total absence of supporting evidence. If there were good supporting evidence, then faith would be superfluous, for the evidence would compel us to believe it anyway.'[18]

Now of course in the limited and particular circumstances of an argument between those who do and those who do not accept the scientific truth of the book of Genesis, this

17 *The Extended Phenotype*, p. 39.
18 *The Selfish Gene*, endnote (p. 330) to p. 198.

distinction between faith and reason makes some sense. But a distinction between rational belief and unmotivated certainty does not coincide with the distinction between science and religion, or even between science and Christianity. Dawkins's confusion between argument and polemical definition is pretty strong evidence against the intrinsic rationality of scientists.

Darwinism does make real difficulties for Christianity.[19] These problems are worth discussing later. But they do not arise from a clash between the differing historical accounts of the creation of life – no one who cares about historical truth can believe the Genesis story literally. Most of the serious, dogged labour in proving Genesis inconsistent with itself, as well as with the geological record, was done by priests; and, in Britain, completed by the time of the trial in 1865 of Bishop Colenso for exactly the heresy of pointing out that Genesis can't be literally true. He was acquitted.

But you would not gather any of this from the Dawkinsians, who persistently write as if the only form of Christianity, and perhaps of religion, ever to exist was the kind that brought a heresy charge against Bishop Colenso. There is a note of extraordinary personal loathing in some of his discussions of Christianity, as if every soul won for Jesus had been torn from the arms of Richard Dawkins: 'A beautiful child close to me, six and the apple of her father's eye, believes that Thomas the Tank Engine really exists. She believes in Father Christmas, and when she grows up her

---

19 An evolutionary account of the history of ideas makes difficulties for *any* institution that believes in the persistence of orthodoxy through time. The difficulties confronting people who look for an essence of Christianity (or Mormonism or Darwinism) are similar, and I think similarly insurmountable, to those confronting people who look for an unchangeable essence to every species.

ambition is to be a tooth fairy. She and her schoolfriends believe the solemn word of respected adults that tooth fairies and Father Christmas really exist. This little girl is of an age to believe whatever you tell her. If you tell her about witches changing princes into frogs she will believe you. If you tell her that bad children roast forever in hell she will have nightmares. I have just discovered that without her father's consent this sweet, trusting, gullible six-year-old is being sent, for weekly instruction, to a Roman Catholic nun. What chance has she?'[20]

Any father can sympathise with this anguish – if it's his own daughter he is describing – just as one can sympathise with Creationist parents who don't want their children taught that morality is nothing more than a trick played on us by selfish genes. But anguish is no guarantee of truth.

Gould, by contrast, displays a sympathy towards religious beliefs and believers which exists independently of the truths of their beliefs. His views of the philosophical consequences of Darwinism are wholly incompatible with the idea of an ordered universe designed for our benefit. He has no time for the 'strong anthropic principle' – an argument favoured by some Christian or otherwise spiritually minded intellectuals which says that it is so unlikely that the universe should have produced us that we can deduce from this unlikelihood that the whole show was produced for our benefit.

'The claim that a conscious creature like us must evolve because we can predict the development of [increasing complexity] for all of life represents a classic category mistake. Increasingly complex animals did predictably arise (if only as a passive consequence) but any individual animal among them at this particular time represents a fortuitous and

20 'Viruses of the Mind'.

improbable result, one actualization among a hundred million unrealized alternatives. Wind the tape of life back to the origin of modern multicellular animals in the Cambrian explosion, let the tape play again from this identical starting point, and the replay will populate the earth . . . with a radically different set of creatures. The chance that this alternative set will contain anything remotely like a human being must be effectively nil, while the probability of any kind of creature endowed with self-consciousness must also be vanishingly small.

'We are global accidents of an unpredictable process with no drive to complexity, not the expected results of evolutionary principles that yearn to produce a creature capable of understanding the mode of its own necessary construction.'[21]

This is a viewpoint opposed to more than just the Christian belief that we are specially significant. In the importance that Gould allows to chance and to contingency, he is also opposed to a great deal of simplistic reductionist confidence that there is a set of rules which explain all the interesting things about the world, and that we have found them. Compare the Oxford chemist and Dawkinsian atheist Peter Atkins, who says that 'A great deal of the universe does not need any explanation. Elephants, for instance. Once molecules have learnt to compete and to create other molecules in their own image, elephants, and things resembling elephants, will in due course be found roaming through the countryside.'[22] Note that this supposedly radical materialism is offered to us in a world-picture in which molecules can 'learn', 'compete', and 'create'. There is

---

21 Slightly modified, from *Life's Grandeur*, p. 214.
22 Quoted in Dawkins, *The Blind Watchmaker*, p. 14.

something very skewed here. The idea that a molecule might be capable of any of these activities is at least as mysterious as the doctrines of the Trinity; yet it is offered as a sort of brusque common sense and demystification. What starts off as an attempt to despiritualise the universe ends up populating it with spirits contending in every molecule.

Gould, like Lewontin, understands American creationism as in part a class issue: it is a way for otherwise despised and marginal people to assert the importance and autonomy of morality in their lives. Social Darwinism in its original Spencerian form was overwhelmingly popular in America (and in imperial Germany before the First World War). In both cases it was an ideology used by the strong to say that their subjugation of the weak was necessary and good. The Social Darwinists stamped round the world like Vogon guards. 'Resistance is useless' was their message to the weak. 'But before I kill you, you must hear my poetry.' Is it any wonder that some victims stopped their ears?

Gould has argued that the early Creationists, especially William Jennings Bryan, were attempting to defend justice against the strong, and that they were right to say that some Darwinian theories were used as implements of exploitation. Of course, Darwinian ideas need not be used in this way. The idea that human suffering can be justified by looking at evolutionary progress will not survive the end of any idea of progress in evolution: and one of the main themes of Gould's work has been that evolution is *not* progressive; and that if it appears to be, this is merely a trick of perspective. Bacteria are still the most numerous, the largest by weight, and perhaps the most influential form of life on the planet, he argues in *Life's Grandeur*.

If evolution were genuinely progressive this, too, would raise horrible moral problems. Suppose it could be shown that there was a tendency to produce ever more morally and intellectually perfect beings. It looks at present as if George Price and his collaborators proved that this cannot be the case and that the process must have limits. But even if this interpretation of sociobiology is wrong,[23] the moral charge against the universe remains. Suppose we assume that morally perfect beings could, and will, evolve: how could they conclude that their existence was worth all the suffering and misery necessary to produce it?

Anyone who believes in the importance of justice and mercy must be worried by Darwinism. When I told Mary Midgley the story of George Price's madness and suicide, she responded, 'At least he saw how important these discoveries are.' The mixture of kin selection and game theory which Price worked on, and which form the backbone of *The Selfish Gene*, really do provide explanations for how co-operative behaviour can arise in the world, how it can spread, and how we can be born with all our good and tender instincts. They are not, as the cynic or stoic might argue, merely self-deception or hypocrisy, any more than hunger is, or lust. This raises again the horrible question of why all these instincts should have appeared in a world that is bound to frustrate them. To that extent there is some truth in the agreement between Darwinians and their opponents that Darwinism is necessarily opposed to Christian certainties.

But did anyone ever really believe in them? I don't think that the questions about the place of justice and mercy in the universe which Darwinism throws into such high relief were ever any more satisfactorily answered by Christianity – or by

---

23 Olaf Stapledon has tried to think out such matters. Try *Last and First Men*.

any other system of belief. If there had ever existed any belief system that could really, lastingly, persuade people that the world is a just and merciful place, I do not see how it could ever have been replaced by any of the alternatives on offer, including Christianity and the other world religions.

The main advantage of well-established religions over new ones is that they have grown better at concealing from us the fact that they don't have answers. Certainly Christianity has no answer to the problem of suffering and evil except in the form of an assurance that God is somehow implicated in it; and even those who accept this assurance find it incomprehensible[24] – as, rather differently, do those who reject it. 'Take, for example, the central claim of all non-heretical versions of Christianity, namely that God is all-powerful and all-loving. People have been sent to the stake for denying one or other of these predicates. Yet an application of elementary logic to the overwhelming factual evidence shows that such a conception of God is downright inconsistent. An all-powerful, all-loving God simply would not allow small children to die in screaming agony – and that is that', writes Michael Ruse, one of the most subtle and interesting philosophers of Darwinism (and, like Gould, one of the witnesses against Creationism in the 1982 Alabama trial).[25]

What is interesting in this context about Ruse's objection to the doctrine of God is that it would lose none of its force if the Creationists were proved right tomorrow; if anything, it would gain power from such a miracle: we could describe as omnipotent a God who gives cancer to children and

---

24 See *Celebration*, by Margaret Spufford, one of the few theologians both able and willing to be intellectually honest.
25 Ruse, *Taking Darwin Seriously*, p. 176.

knowledge of the truth to Ian Paisley, but we should not call Him loving or just. The moral case against God was nowhere put with greater ferocity and force than by Voltaire in *Candide*, before Darwin's grandfather was born.

If science has indeed made human life better – as everyone in these arguments would agree it has – it has simultaneously made Dr Pangloss seem more credible: at least, it has removed from our contemplation the more immediate disproofs of his optimism. The varieties of suffering and of the sheer gut-wrenching wrongness of the world which are in modern societies kept in the shadowed calm of a children's surgical ward can be seen every day on the pavements of really poor countries, and could no doubt be seen all over Europe before the Industrial Revolution. Voltaire was not the first to notice these horrors. Job was. Even Jesus was heard to cry out, 'My God, my God, why have you forsaken me?'

No doubt the question could truly be answered by pointing out that the God in question does not exist. But this response is wholly inadequate to the anguish of the question, which gains its terrible force from the fact that it is, in a sense, unaffected by the truth of the answer. It goes on being asked. It is built into our structure. We have moral appetites just as truly as we have bestial ones: and they are just as much condemned to ultimate frustration.

This is the hideous fork on which George Price was impaled and from which neither Darwinism nor Christianity could rescue him. Both can explain how this mismatch between our longings and the world around us came about. Neither can abolish it.

It is characteristic of atheists to overestimate the comfort that religious belief is supposed to bring to believers. Partly, of course, this is because it allows us to pose as heroic, clear-sighted, and able to dispense with all those pathetic fictions. But when I look at them as dispassionately as possible, Christians, in my experience, do not really believe in heaven or hell. They would not be so often enjoined to have hope if hope were easy or even always possible.

I never see the ones that I know behaving like people who really believe that once they have died, an eternity of bliss awaits them and everyone they love.[26] And it is a matter of demonstrable historical fact that religions can exist without any clear doctrine of the afterlife, and that even those religions which now have clear and worked-out doctrines of one started without any hope of personal immortality (Islam excepted, but then it is a fairly late development). Religions did not, *pace* Freud, come into being to help us cope with the shock of realising our own mortality, though they may make it easier to bear the death of people we love.

In fact it is tempting to argue that, though Christianity appears to derive from a succession of lies – there was no Garden, no Fall, no Adam and no Eve; Jesus's body was not resurrected – it may have produced more useful truths than Darwinism even though Darwinism's story is true. Christianity has done a much better job of assimilating its insights into human nature into rules of conduct, which can stand independently of the pictures from which they are derived.

Pop Darwinism nowadays supplies the language, the imagery, and the over-arching story with which people discuss theological questions. There is a perfect example in this morning's *Guardian* as I write. Professor Harold Kroto,

---

26 Plenty of them live as if this life were but an empty dream, an illusion, or a vale of tears to be hurried through; but that need not be evidence of a surfeit of faith so much as of a shortage of Prozac.

who has won a Nobel Prize for Chemistry and may therefore be presumed to know something about science, writes that 'The truly beautiful and wonderful discovery of Darwin, that all living creatures are related, has made not a scrap of difference to man's inhumanity to man.' But why should it? The truly beautiful and wonderful discoveries of Hamilton and Price and Maynard Smith have gone on from Darwin to show that a world where all living things are related will come to be populated by creatures that can discriminate among their relatives, and which favour those closest to them at the expense of all others.

The beauty and wonder and truth of scientific theories all are real. But there is no logical link from them to a benevolent ethic, any more than there is a logical link between the omnipotence of God and His love for His creation. The problem with this connection between morality and evolution is that moral or metaphysical positions are presented in scientific language. Perhaps this is an attempt to give them an impersonal and normative character which would render them objective and independent of human whims: it seems to belong to the character of a moral law that it should be true even if we don't want to believe it. Once religious belief is seen as optional, the only body of belief which goes on being true whether we like it or not is science; so ethics is fitted into a scientific rather than a religious universe. But the fit there is just as bad as it was in the bad old days of superstition.

Again and again, when examining the relationship between evolutionary doctrine and ethics, I am struck by the way in which the absence of any logical connection seems to do nothing to diminish the desire for an emotional relationship. Never mind the logical impossibility of deducing 'ought' from 'is': what gives popular arguments about

Darwinism so much fervour is the way they make it easy to go in the other direction, from 'is' to 'ought'.[27]

This is not the argument that religion knows about ethics, whereas science knows about facts. At least, it is not quite the same argument. The point is that for science to spread as an explanation through society, it must come tangled with, perhaps animated by, an ethical theory and an account of our place in the universe. Pure science may know about facts quite free of values,[28] but pop science is a matter of facts and values all tangled together until they make some kind of common sense.

This is certainly true in Western Europe, where the popularity of pop science is greatest in the most secular countries. For the extraordinary thing about the pop-science-book market is that it is not driven by scientific curiosity at all. What people want is science which appears to answer religious questions. This means physics, cosmology and biology. There are no works of popular chemistry.[29] Successful science publishers know this perfectly well: a noticeable theme in science books is that they should take religious titles, though these had better not be too explicit. *The God Particle* bombed. *Does God Play Dice* and *God and the New Physics* did better; Dawkins is unable to resist titles that give a religious reverberation to his pronouncements: *River out of Eden, Immortal Coils*.

Science can constrain religious theories, and will certainly affect the kind of language in which they can be expressed. But it cannot specify them. For example, the statement that 'God loved us before we loved him' – or even that 'all men

---

27 Or, for pop sociobiology, from 'ought' to 'was'.
28 Or possibly not.
29 Though you can still make money out of textbooks.

are brothers' – is at bottom an assertion of the fundamental benevolence of the universe, which survives in that sense long after the supporting structure has been stripped away. As such, I think it is one which it is wise to accept, if only because, as Mary Midgley has pointed out, the opposite assertion is hard to combine with sanity. Of course this is not a scientific judgement. But neither is the assertion that the universe is radically malign. Our reasons for choosing between them cannot be scientific either.

Yet the choice is one which matters immensely to people. One can explain this in many ways: perhaps it is a fundamental feature of our make-up to want to know that we are on the winning side, and if we can grasp the universe as a concept, we want to know that we are on the wining side in that. Since science now has the prestige, both socially and intellectually, that religion once had, as a means of divining truth and taming power, we want these assertions to be made in scientific language. Just how difficult this desire has been to eradicate, even for highly trained scientists, may be seen in the views of Julian Huxley, one of the founders of neo-Darwinism, who was none the less able to believe in some kind of progress as a law of life. He wrote in 1926:

'We cannot say that evolution is purposeful until we are privileged to know what processes occur in the thought of God; but we can and must say that it has *direction*. On average, the upper level of biological attainment has been continually raised. Not only this, but our own standards, moral, aesthetic, and intellectual alike, have been produced by this process, and tend to continue the direction of evolution in the future along the line it has followed in the past – towards "more life". That being so, we must say that those actions which tend to help the advance of the upper level of living matter – today represented by man – along a continuation of the line it has followed in the past, are *good*; while those which tend to hinder it are *bad*.'[30]

It is this kind of optimism, not Christian hope, which has been the main victim of changing understandings of Darwinism since George Price's work: but it has been rejected as much by the Gouldians as by the Dawkinsians. Huxley's attempts to find a pattern and a comfort in the process of evolution do not survive selfish genery; but they are just as much confuted by the calculations Gould quotes to establish the importance and success of bacteria. Perhaps more so, since there is no temptation to regard bacteria as the puppet-masters of all that happens on earth.

Yet Huxley went on to write that 'Through evolution, moral values become entwined with verifiable facts outside the sphere of human life.'[31] Though the particular entanglement he thought he saw has been rejected, the connection between evolution and morality remains intimate. The fear that has haunted Europe at least since Machiavelli is that morality is no more than a social convention which we are free to accept or reject. One of the messages of sociobiology is that this must be wrong: we are not actually the sort of animal that is free to accept or reject social conventions; and that such a species could not in fact evolve.[32] Of course, in any particular instance, and at the scale of the individual, we do make moral choices every day; and we might be thought to reject whole moral systems with every choice we make.

---

30 *Essays in Popular Science*, Julian Huxley.

31 Ibid.

32 Individual animals of this sort might appear in a generally social species. We call them sociopaths. But it's not clear that a sociopath can really choose to feel the kind of moral obligations we do.

But, however many we destroy or reject, we seem unable to avoid constructing new ones, and fitting them into the universe. Whether this is a spandrel or an exaptation must be left as an exercise to the reader.

10

REPLICATION IS NOT ENOUGH

MOST OF THIS book has been concerned with scientists doing philosophy more or less badly, with occasional diversions to watch philosophers attempting science.

But in the background there are always scientists doing science (like Price and Maynard Smith) and there have also been philosophers other than Dennett and Mary Midgley trying to do philosophy in the light of Darwin. The most interesting of these attempts have nothing to do with moral philosophy. The paradoxes of human goodness and justice in a bad and unjust world had been around for millennia before game theory or population genetics was applied to them. The selfish and wicked features of our nature are the same whether we explain them by a fall from Eden or the workings of natural selection on a social species of primate.

Moral philosophy is what has made most of the fuss because it is much more interesting and important than science. Most of the world's population have lived, and do live, to the best of their abilities innocent of science. Everybody does moral philosophy every day, if only on a practical level. What is more, it is a subject on which everyone is a critic, and anyone who displeases enough critics stands in real danger. It's hard to think of anyone who has been killed or even beaten up for their scientific opinions. Galileo, it is true, was badly frightened, but no more; other examples are scarce: in 1791 the chemist Joseph Priestley had his house burnt by a mob in Birmingham; but that was because he was a Unitarian, not because of his views on oxygen. From Socrates onwards, however, philosophy has been a dangerous profession. Hundreds of thousands of people at least, and probably millions, have been killed for having the wrong theological opinions or, under atheist regimes, for having any theological opinions at all. Scientific theories, however mistaken or correct, will at worst bring you the contempt and opprobrium of other scientists.

But Darwinism has large implications for the philosophy of science. As well as the vulgar knockabout stuff on memes, knowledge, and religion which the previous chapter covered, there have also been some serious and sophisticated attempts to ask what a really Darwinian world would look like, and what sort of processes would be important in it. Chief among these is David Hull's *Science as a Process*, published in 1988, which is partly an enquiry into whether ideas might undergo a Darwinian process in the way that science is actually done. Though he dislikes the word, it might be thought of as a search for the memes of science. It is a fat book, scrupulously detailed and full of sly jokes, starting with the cover, on which a large group of naked men are trying to kill each other with bows, swords and axes. Their expressions are gleeful; most of the scientists in his photographs look miserable or uneasy, perhaps because they are being unnaturally polite.

If you want to understand exactly what Darwinian explanations are, and what they can be used to explain, this is by far the most scrupulous and illuminating book on the market. It is not just an illumination of biology. If there could ever be a 'science of memetics', this would be its founding text.

Though his narrative deals briefly with the early struggles over sociobiology, most of his case history is derived from a series of quarrels even more arcane and vicious, among rival schools of taxonomists. Whereas the sociobiologists are arguing about large questions of human freedom and purpose, Hull describes a world in which grown men can quarrel for life about the distribution of midges in the Antarctic. There is – obviously – some overlap with other fields of evolutionary biology. But for the most part the quarrels he describes serve to show that there is nothing uniquely unpleasant about the way that evolutionary biologists or philosophers treat each other.

Classification and theories of evolution are intimately linked, because theories of classification specify what it is that evolves and where it evolves to: a classification scheme in which species are fixed and immutable has no place for Darwinian change between them. And once the fact of evolution is admitted, the rate and direction can be assessed only if we can decide what species exist, and how they are to be related to each other. These problems are not nearly as simple as they look.

In the 1950s the dominant school of taxonomy tried to classify animals and plants in ways that would show both their similarities and their place in the family trees that record the history of evolution. But two schools, later known as cladists and pheneticists, arose to challenge this ambition. Both proposed to ignore historical explanations and to discover what could be learnt by looking at the world with fresh eyes, as if we did not need to slot things into an evolutionary history. This was a paradoxical tribute to the strength and coherence of evolutionary explanations, though duly misrepresented by Creationists. The fact of evolution is so well established that one could safely leave the choice of particular stories of evolution in the air.

The battles between these various schools were as savage as anything in the playground. Hull wrote that 'in reading six years of referees' reports for *Systematic Zoology* I was struck by the gratuitous nastiness that characterised so many of the reviews . . . for example, one referee . . . agreed with the message of the manuscript but concluded that the author's writing style had all the flair of picking one's nose and eating the snot.'[1] He has a culturally adaptationist explanation for this, too. The moment at which a manuscript goes out is the moment of an author's greatest vulnerability. That is obviously the moment to put the boot in if you are competing with him for fame among your peers, which Hull takes to be one of the fundamental motives of science.

Hull took Dawkins's original discussion of selection processes in *The Selfish Gene* and turned it on its head so deftly and politely that he caused no fuss. In Dawkins, the genes (and memes) function as replicators, and their products are vehicles. The three properties that a gene – or anything like it – must have to function in a selection process, are longevity, fecundity, and fidelity. Replicators must be copied many times: they must be copied accurately, though not with perfect accuracy, and in large numbers. When these three conditions are met, we can expect some replicators to be copied more often and to become more frequent than others. All this Hull agrees with and praises. However, he takes Dawkins's idea of vehicles – the bodies that genes build and use to contend with each other – and turns it into something independently important. Instead of 'vehicles' he

---

1 *Science as a Process*, p. 325.

talks about 'interactors'; and it is they, not the genes or replicators, which drive the process of evolution forward.

For Hull, theories are replicators, and scientists are inter- actors. How does this differ from the theory that humans are passive vectors for meme infestation? Some people can't see the difference. I have seen his theory described as making scientists simply the vehicles of their theories. But 'vehicles' is Dawkins's term. It has quite different connotations, and so a meaning that is not the same as 'interactors'. For Hull the interactors are active participants in the process. In fact, they drive it. Selection he defines as 'a process in which the differential extinction and proliferation of interactors *cause* the differential perpetuation of the relevant replicators' (the italics are Hull's).[2]

For Dawkins, on the other hand, the replicators cause everything to happen. A body is only 'a communal *vehicle* for replicators. A vehicle is an entity in which replicators (genes and memes) travel about, an entity whose attributes are affected by the replicators inside it, an entity which may be seen as a compound tool of replicator propagation.'[3] It doesn't, in other words, *do* anything. 'A nest, like a bird, is a gene's way of making another gene.'[4]

Perhaps this difference of emphasis can be made clearer by looking at life as a casino, in the metaphor of Jacques Monod. At Dawkins's table, the genes are playing. Their cards represent body shapes, behaviour. The genes play these cards in competition with each other; after each deal the cards are swept away and only the genes remain. At Hull's table, the players are the organisms, doing the best they can

---

2 Ibid, p. 409.
3 *The Extended Phenotype*, p. 112.
4 Ibid, p. 98.

with the genes they have been dealt. The outcome of the game depends on the relationship between the players as much as it does on the cards. Of course, it has nothing to do with Lamarckianism. Hull is not saying that organisms can change their own genes: rather that it is the lives of organisms which determine the fate of their genes.

This view also has consequences when we look at the spread and evolution of ideas. In the context of cultural evolution one need not take 'extinction' and 'proliferation' literally. Scientists spread their beliefs by means other than copulation, and defeat their enemies without killing them. The same scientist can act as the interactor for different groups of replicators when he changes his mind. But the distinction between being an interactor and being a vehicle is that a scientist's actions, carried out for reasons possibly quite independent of his beliefs, become indispensable in spreading them. It also cuts out all the nonsense about 'meme victims'.

This is a very social view of the way in which science progresses, for it sees the spread of scientific ideas as the consequence of interactions among scientists. Though charm alone is not enough to get ideas accepted, it helps; and a sufficiently unattractive and quarrelsome personality is almost enough to ensure that even brilliant ideas are ignored by other people working in the field, a point Hull illustrates with copious examples.

This process of social construction is not unconstrained. Hull is careful to analyse the social barriers and tabus necessary for a community of scientists actually to make scientific progress. Amongst other things, he points out that they must trust one another's work. As against Humphrey's picture of science as an open and transparent process, where understanding of what has been done is freely available, Hull points out that all scientists are building constantly on work they have not done and may not understand. That is partly why cheating, when it is detected, is punished so severely: because one false experiment may wreck the work of many other scientists who have relied on it. Cheating in science is the equivalent of cowardice in the armed forces. It is the vice or weakness that most threatens the whole enterprise. Equally, being trusted and publicly credited is the reward that scientists hope for.

Hull, like Dennett, was trying to come up with a general model of Darwinian processes, which would apply as much to ideas as to living things. Unlike Dennett, he concluded that the relationship between a thing and the role it plays is problematical. To be a 'gene' or an 'interactor' is not, for him, an intrinsic quality of DNA, but a consequence of the roles it plays. From this it follows that the same piece of DNA can be playing distinct, overlapping and even contradictory roles at the same time; and this insight leads to the lapidary sentence at the heart of his book: 'The idea is as much of a myth as the gene.' For the model of something that can play distinct, overlapping, and contradictory roles at the same time is a word, or a thing made out of words.

Perhaps I am wrong to draw too sharp a line here between Hull and the Dawkinsians. His distinction is certainly implicit in their definition and they might accept it, at least in some moods. But he sees it as far more important. And, whereas Dawkins sees the gene as a unit in principle as variable as Hull does – and remarks that his book could just as well be called 'The Selfish Fuzzy Chromosomal Unit' – he seems to think that its important function is to be copied, whereas to Hull the copying makes no sense without the winnowing. It is not enough to replicate. Other things must interact.

That is why his definitions of both replicators and inter-actors are based on the role they play. The first half of this move had been anticipated: the definition of an analytical gene first offered by George Williams, and later used by all the sociobiologists, is precisely 'any length of chromosome that acts like a gene'. But the idea of an organism or an animal seems so self-evident that a fancy definition is unnecessary.

Dawkins argued in *The Extended Phenotype* that an animal's body is not the simple and self-evident thing that it appears to be. It may be controlled by another animal's genes. Parasites, for example, can have profound physiological effects on their hosts. They can make the host behave in ways that are suicidal for it, yet excellent for the parasite. An example (mine, not his) of this sort of process would be the way that tobacco plants cause humans to plant them though they are bad for us, or at least for our bodies. If you regard the leaves of a tobacco plant simply as an expression of its genes, why should you not regard the inside of a smoker's lungs, or the state of the neurochemicals in his brain, in a similar light, as expressions of tobacco genes upon the world?

Or, if that seems far-fetched, and to involve complicated questions of human free will, there is a peculiarly horrible and brilliant example quoted in *The Extended Phenotype* (p. 216) of a minute worm which parasitises freshwater shrimps[5] at one stage in its life and ducks at a later stage. When startled, shrimps infected with this parasite swim towards the surface, where they are more vulnerable to the ducks that eat them, whereas uninfected shrimps and those infected by another, similar parasite, which prefers diving duck species as its final

---

5 *Gammarus.* They're not really shrimps; but if trout don't discriminate, why should we?

host, both dive when they are startled, and both prefer darkness to the light of shallow water.

The shrimp's body, Dawkins argues, is here doing things that are good for the parasite's genes, not for the shrimp's; so (if bodies are controlled by genes) we should think of it as belonging to the parasite's genes rather than the shrimp's. For Dawkins, there is a simple one-way power relationship between genes and the bodies they build, so the struggle for the shrimp's behaviour is best understood as a struggle between contending genes. One of the effects of exploding the concept of the body in this way is to increase the importance of the gene: this might not follow from necessity, since even extended phenotypes must interact, but these interactions become so complicated that the temptation to ignore them is sometimes overwhelming.

Just as Hull inverted the relative importance of replicators and interactors, he similarly transformed the concept of memes. For the Dawkinsian, a meme is something that lives inside the brain. There it behaves analogously to a gene. Behaviours that the meme produces – whether speech, humming tunes, or a tendency to froth at the mouth whenever the Pope is mentioned – are then considered as phenotypes: things the meme has made in order to spread itself.[6]

For Hull, the replicator – he avoids the term 'meme' – is the external, embodied idea. If it has a phenotypic stage, this takes place inside a scientist's mind. 'Scientists themselves are anything but passive vehicles. Without scientists, no conceptual replicator [idea] could ever be tested, and testing is essential to science.'[7]

---

6 Note that it is very hard to talk about this without ascribing agency to memes. It's not surprising that believers see their opponents as possessed.
7 *Science as a Process*, p. 478.

Perhaps these definitions seem abstruse and metaphysical. But metaphysics matters, not because it is difficult and abstract, but because it is terribly easy and closely entangled with everything practical. As Mary Midgley remarks, 'Anyone can commit an act of metaphysics. The difficulty is to extricate yourself from the consequences.'[8]

So, having sorted out his metaphysics, Hull set out to make a model of cultural evolution that would stand up to the criticisms levelled against memes. The most obvious of these criticisms, of course, is that memes don't actually exist. There are two ways around this. The first, as we have seen, was to place his replicators outside the brain. There is no need to argue that this book is transmitting invisible little wriggly ideas from my mind to yours – or that the little wriggly ideas forced my brain to make this book. All his idea requires is that there should be a process by which the ideas in this book are transmitted by readers. If they're not transmitted they disappear. That's fine. It happens to genes, too.

The second reason for supposing that memes don't exist is that they seem to disappear as soon as you look at them closely. Anything offered as a 'meme' turns out to be made out of other memes, and they, in turn, are made out of others – and so on and on in an infinite regress. Nowhere do we come to the simple building blocks of thought; the elementary particles of cultural transmission. To this Hull responds that genes are just as problematical: memes are not simple chunks of understanding, but neither are genes simple chunks of DNA. 'If one conceives of genes as discrete beads on a string, as they were pictured for one brief moment in the history of genetics, then of course nothing in socio-cultural evolution answers to them, but nothing answers to

---

8 'Selfish Genes and Social Darwinism'.

them in biological evolution either . . . The "idea" is as much of a myth as the "gene".[9]

In fact, he says, simple chunks of understanding can't exist. 'There are no atomic sentences, no atomic facts, and no one-to-one correspondence between the two. Our understanding of the world cannot be subdivided into units of equal size and treated in isolation from other conceptual units.'[10] This has the incidental and surely desirable effect of abolishing the whole idea of 'meme swarms': memeticists argue that complex conceptual systems, like religions, are somehow built up from ensembles of simpler ones. Instead of claiming that religions are composed of a mixture of intolerance and gullibility, which might seem to impose on readers' gullibility and tolerance, they prefer to explain that religions are the product of an evolutionary disposition to believe what your parents tell you, coupled with a meme that says doubt is dangerous and another meme that says the people who disagree with you will go to hell. This, apparently, is the scientific method.

The other major objection raised to cultural evolution is that it is 'Lamarckian', or at least blending. In some forms, this objection is a recognition of the obvious fact that we affect the ideas we transmit, as we do not affect our genes.[11] My ideas change as a result of my life experiences. I transmit only the ones that work. I am able to some extent to direct

---

9 *Science as a Process*, pp. 442–3.

10 Ibid.

11 Quite soon, of course, it will become possible, as a result of cultural evolution, for us to decide which physical genes we want to transmit to our children. But that was not in the minds of the people who raised this objection and is irrelevant to the traditional distinction between 'Darwinian' and 'Lamarckian' evolution (as, indeed, are the factual beliefs of Darwin and Lamarck).

the evolution of my ideas. But this, says Hull, is not Lamarckianism, which would require that my ideas somehow directly influence my genes. 'In the only sense in which conceptual replicators are characteristics, they are not inherited; in the only sense in which they are inherited, they are not characteristics.'[12] Indirect influence is not here an issue. Culture does influence gene flow, but only because it alters the environment we find ourselves in, and thus the adaptive value of particular genes.

If ideas can directly influence only other ideas, this influence is simply an example of recombination among replicators, which we would expect in any selective system. This recombination is often drastic. But Hull argues that biological recombination is often drastic, too, providing we remember that most living things are not animals and certainly not vertebrates. Ideas, in his scheme, are more like vegetables than viruses. They can be made to bear very strange fruits, just as plants can be genetically modified to sweat plastics.

The gains from all this abstraction are considerable. It becomes possible for a historian of ideas to act like a palaeontologist of culture, tracing the rise and extinction of new conceptual worlds. It also becomes possible to treat ideas, like species, as historically existing entities, with a beginning and an end. Conceptual systems, in Hull's view, are like species in another very important respect: they have no essence. Not only are the boundaries of a species necessarily fuzzy, but a species turns out in Darwin's world to have no centre. There is no platonic perfect type of a particular animal or plant, of which all others are more or less imperfect copies. This is one reason why taxonomists have

---

12 *Science as a Process*, p. 454.

got so much to argue about. But it is also necessary. Removing the fixity of species is necessary if they are to change into each other. To the Bible believer who argues that God made every living thing 'after its kind', the Darwinian replies that even if omnipotent, He could not have done, because He made no kinds for animals to be after.

Applying this reasoning to the history of ideas, Hull concludes that 'Darwinism no more has an essence than does Copernicanism, sociobiology, or Christianity for that matter, protestations by their advocates and opponents notwithstanding.'[13] This is not to say that there are no beliefs one can identify as Darwinian, Christian or whatever: only that it is an important part of this identification to specify who held them in what context, and when. Of all the subversions that Darwinism can make of religious beliefs, this seems to me the subtlest and the most profound. It removes from our contemplation eternal truths and replaces them with time-bound and mortal beliefs.

Another point about this abstraction from the wriggly bits is that it lets one study the transmission of meaning, rather than information. Instead of being intrinsic to its representation, meaning emerges only in context. We have already seen how genes form a language – flexible, context-dependent, and impossible to traverse backwards, so that you cannot get from the thing described to the one and only correct description. They are built, on the other hand, from a rigid code: given a particular sequence of amino acids, we know which sequences of DNA could have produced it.[14]

---

13 Ibid, p. 207.
14 We don't know exactly which one of those sequences, because there is some redundancy in the code.

In Hull's model, languages work like languages, too, and not like codes. The same stretch of words can belong in entirely different lineages of argument – which is another way of putting the overwhelmingly obvious and important point that a string of words can have different meanings, none of which is intrinsically essential or right. It follows that the flow of meanings through society must to some extent be studied independently of the use of language, so that if you are tracking the spread of a phrase or word, such as 'meme' or 'selfish gene', you are in each case tracking the spread of several different and sometimes incompatible ideas. Conversely, if you want to study the spread of an idea, you must analyse the use of language very closely. It's not clear how a memeticist should choose between these two projects, but he or she must choose.

The ideas Hull is describing correspond entirely to analytical genes. They are units of cultural heredity, not – as analogues to functional genes would be – instructions for building thoughts. By doing this he is able to model a selection process that sides-steps all the obvious objections to memes; but it delivers almost nothing of what they promise. Not even the most fervent anti-memeticist would deny the analogies between culture and biology. Of course cultural evolution proceeds by descent with modification – to use Darwin's phrase. Of course you can trace the family trees of ideas or languages. Of course some specialised forms of culture show adaptation and improvement: improvements in human technology are in an important sense analogous to the improvements in an animal's body or behavioural repertoire. But the promise of memes is that they might provide a particular *mechanism* for all this, in the way that genetics has provided a mechanism for Darwinian change; and that is the promise that Hull has broken.

By sorting carefully through all the ways in which culture is and is not like biology, Hull has provided what is probably the best model of selection processes in culture that we are going to get; it is a curiously disappointing one.

Instead of a throbbing drama of memes and genes with their blind, virus-like purposiveness, there is a sort of palaeontology of culture. It tells us little interesting about the future. Neither, of course, does evolutionary theory. That is one of the things that are meant by calling it 'blind' and 'impersonal'. There are no general laws of progress in biological evolution. There seem to be in science and in other forms of human knowledge. This need not mean that science is not an evolutionary process. It may be simply that we are comparing two things at very different scales. When you look at the details of natural selection, there is tremendous progress: providing the problem stays constant and important, natural selection can refine solutions to an extraordinary extent until it develops such marvels of sophistication as an ant's brain or the dentition of a pike.

Since the world that scientists are trying to understand remains constant – there are laws of Nature – and since understanding it will always be hugely important, it is hardly surprising that science as a whole can be progressive and can steadily increase its store of reliable knowledge. But these general principles won't tell us where in particular knowledge will next increase, nor how.

Having general laws does not predict the particular instances that will obey them. This makes a difficulty for any selective account of culture, not just Hull's. This is not immediately apparent because he has confined his enquiry to science – at least, to scientific concepts. Within these confines it is reasonably easy to identify the concepts and ideas whose history he wants to trace. Scientists in a particular discipline all use language in more or less the same way, and when they disagree about the meaning of important words they have no difficulty in making the fact of disagreement clear, even if its matter remains recalcitrant to enquiry.

But as soon as this kind of language enters the wider world, it loses almost all precision. Multiple, overlapping simultaneous meanings are the fated freight of any phrase in general use. One can see this very clearly with the central ideas of selfish genery. Sociobiology spread so rapidly partly through the personification of the gene, though a real price was paid in understanding once genes were given attributes like selfishness and set free to roam the world on their own. However, what lay behind the idea of the selfish gene was a clear and mathematically expressible reality: any particular discussion of the selfishness or altruism of genes can always be translated back to see if it makes sense as a description of actual changes in the world. You *can* sometimes safely call genes selfish, simply because a moment's thought shows that they can't possibly be.

Similar considerations apply to other ideas, such as gene-centrism. The idea of gene-centred evolution can be understood in two separate ways. It can be used as a way to examine the change of gene frequencies within a population – this is strict neo-Darwinism. Say, a mutation arises among rabbits which permits them to run faster: it spreads rapidly through the population at the expense of slower-running rabbits, who are more often caught by foxes. One can perfectly well see this as the consequence of the spread of a particular allele through the rabbit population. One form of rabbit gene is replacing another. This is not a controversial description.

At the end of the process, the weary foxes find that all the remaining rabbits now run faster than hares. So they switch to eating hares instead. The rabbit population rises, and the hare population falls. The second form of gene-centrism is to say that what is really happening here is the replacement of hare DNA by rabbit DNA. But this is startlingly uninformative. It doesn't offer any explanation of why the replacement should have occurred: any such explanation would involve the interactions of foxes with hares and rabbits. Similar reasoning can be applied to the case of the tobacco genes contending through their effects in human brains. It is true that if you are interested in book-keeping among the tobacco genes,[15] and in discovering which ones will spread through the population, the answer to these questions will be found in the effects they have on human tissue, rather than on tobacco leaves. But this is no reason for being interested in tobacco genes in the first place. Just because some interactions in human tissue are important to their fate does not mean that the genes determine these interactions. Gene-centrism in that sense retreats into a kind of mysticism. That's not to say it's useless: simply that it should be judged on its merits as mysticism – a picture of the world, perhaps a beautiful and awe-inspiring one, but not an explanation.

The threat of sociobiology, or evolutionary psychology, is usually considered to lie in the way that it makes us less than human by reducing everything to genes. One way to look at the transition from early sociobiology to modern evolutionary psychology is that it has grown steadily less gene-centric and more sophisticated about the kind of things that genes can be expected to do. There are exceptions. There is Steven Pinker. But judged by the standards of the most

---

15 That is, recording and tracking the spread of rival alleles through the population.

thorough, scrupulous, and incidentally devastating, critique of early sociobiology, Philip Kitcher's book *Vaulting Ambition*, it has done pretty well.

This will not stop people believing that their genes control everything, any more than it will stop them believing in astrology. But at least there is no scientific warrant for either belief. The real mistake is a deeper and more general one. It is to believe not in the tyranny of the genes, but in the tyranny of the replicators. This is true whether these replicators are conceived of as genes, as strategies of behaviour, or as ideas. The discovery of ways in which all these things can work as replicators has been one of the great intellectual triumphs of the last fifty years. It really is wonderful, exciting, and all the other things that Richard Dawkins says (and shows) it is. But replication is not enough for a selective process. Genes are selected through bodies, strategies through social animals, and ideas through people. You cannot, if you are to describe the world, stick with only one half of the process.

This is especially true if you try to describe the social world that humans live in, or to answer questions such as 'What is the place of goodness in a Darwinian world?' The beginning of an answer is that goodness is a property of interactors, not of replicators. The more fuss you make about genes, the less you can see the places where goodness is possible. This is not because genes make people behave selfishly, nor even because they make people behave unselfishly, although they predispose us to do both things. But genes themselves cannot behave at all. Behaviour is a property of replicators, bodies, living things.

Thinking that only replicators – or genes – matter, and that interactions can safely be ignored, is misleading about us in another way. For it suggests that the replicators which made us have a single purpose. 'We are . . . robot vehicles blindly programmed to preserve the selfish molecules known as genes' as the infamous passage in *The Selfish Gene* proclaims. Matt Ridley quotes this in *The Origins of Virtue* next to his summary of Hamilton's discovery: 'not only was the human being just another animal but it was also the disposable plaything and tool of a committee of self-interested genes' (p. 19).

What Hamilton actually wrote in this context was rather different in emphasis. 'In life, what was it I really wanted? My own conscious and seemingly indivisible self was turning out far from what I had imagined and I need not be so ashamed of my self-pity! I was an ambassador ordered abroad by some fragile coalition, a bearer of conflicting orders from the uneasy masters of a divided empire. Still baffled about the very nature of the policies I was supposed to support, I was being asked to act, and to act at once – to analyse, report on, influence the world about me. Given my realization of an eternal disquiet within, couldn't I feel better about my own inability to be consistent in what I was doing, about my indecision in matters ranging from daily trivialities up to the very nature of right and wrong?'[16]

An ambassador has freedom; a machine has not. Dawkins (and Ridley) seems to be arguing that the prime directive is 'Do what is best for your genes.' Hamilton sees that this is unworkable, if only because the genes themselves will always have conflicting interests. It might indeed be a great relief to cast off all our worries and moralities, and simply, clear-eyed, serve the omnipotent genome. But we cannot. The road is closed by the nature of natural selection: either

---

16 *Narrow Roads of Gene Land*, p. 135; quoted in Ridley, *The Origins of Virtue*, p. 19.

our genes contain no directions for us, or, if they do, these directions will conflict because all the interesting ones are being selected between. To that extent, Dr Johnson was simply wrong when he wrote, 'He who makes a beast of himself gets rid of the pain of being a man.'[17] The triumph of the gene has made beasts of all of us, but has shown by this that the pain of being human is inescapable. Neither Gods nor Genes can take it away from us.

In this context, George Price looks rather less than mad to believe in a God who shared this pain even if He could neither diminish it nor even save Price from suicide. Certainly the Church was no use to him. At Price's funeral, the preacher told his grieving, bewildered, tiny congregation that 'The trouble with George was that he took his Christianity too seriously.' At this Hamilton rebuked him: 'I think George felt that if it was good enough for St Paul, it was good enough for him.'

Of course, out of context, this can look like a sort of lunacy; but nothing makes sense outside its context – not words, nor beliefs, nor genes. The equation for altruism that drove Price mad makes very little sense on its own; but it might as well stand as his epitaph. So here it is.

$$\overline{w}\Delta\bar{z} = Cov(w,z) = \beta_{wz}V_z$$

---

17 'Anecdotes of the Reverend Percival Stockdale', reprinted in *Johnsonian Miscellanies*, ed George Birbeck Hill (Oxford, 1897). The cause of becoming a beast was 'over-indulgence in drink'.

SOURCES AND FURTHER READING

Aeschylus, *The Eumenides*, in *The Oresteian Trilogy*, trans. Philip Vellacott, rev. edn. (Harmondsworth: Penguin, 1959)

Ardrey, Robert, *African Genesis* (London: Collins, 1961)

Atkins, Peter, *The Creation* (Oxford: W. H. Freeman, 1981)

Chagnon, Napoleon, in *The Genetics of Criminal and Anti-social Behaviour*, ed. Gregory Bock and Jamie A. Goode (London: CIBA Foundation, 1995)

Cronin, Helena, *The Ant and the Peacock: Altruism and Sexual Selection from Darwin to Today* (Cambridge: Cambridge University Press, 1991)

Daly, Martin, and Margo Wilson, *Ethnology and Sociobiology*, vol. 3, pp. 69–78.

— 'The Man who Mistook his Wife for a Chattel', in John Tooby, Jerome H. Barkow and Leda Cosmides, eds., *The Adapted Mind* (Oxford: Oxford University Press, 1995), pp. 289–322

Dawkins, Richard, *The Extended Phenotype* (Oxford: W. H. Freeman, 1982)

— *The Selfish Gene*, 2nd edn., paperback (Oxford and New York: Oxford University Press, 1989; 1st edn. published 1976)

— 'In Defence of Selfish Genes', *Philosophy*, vol. 56 (Cambridge University Press, 1981), pp. 556–73

— *The Blind Watchmaker* (London: Penguin, 1988)

— 'Viruses of the Mind', *Dennett and His Critics: Demystifying Mind*, ed Bo Dahlbom (Cambridge, Mass: 1993)

— *River out of Eden* (London: Weidenfeld & Nicolson, 1995)

Dawson, Doyne, 'The Origins of War: Biological and Anthropological Theories', *History and Theory*, vol. 35 (1996), no. 1

Dennett, Daniel, *Consciousness Explained* (London: Penguin, 1993)

— *Darwin's Dangerous Idea: Evolution and the Meanings of Life* (London: Allen Lane, 1995)

— *Brainchildren* (London: Penguin, 1998)

Evans, Christopher, *The Mighty Micro* (London: Gollancz, 1979)

Fisher, R. A., *The Genetical Theory of Natural Selection* (Oxford: Clarendon Press, 1930)

Frank, Steven, 'George Price's Contributions to Evolutionary Biology', *Journal of Theoretical Biology*, vol. 175 (1995), pp. 373–88; also at http://www.bio.uci.edu/units/ee/faculty/frank.html

Ghiselin, Michael, *Triumph of the Darwinian Method* (Berkeley: University of California Press, 1973)

— *The Economy of Nature and the Evolution of Sex* (Berkeley: University of California Press, 1974)

Gould, Stephen Jay, *Wonderful Life: The Burgess Shale and the Nature of History* (New York: W. W. Norton, 1989)

— *Hen's Teeth and Horse's Toes* (London: Penguin, 1990)

— *The Panda's Thumb: More Reflections in National History* (London: Penguin, 1990)

— *The Flamingo's Smile* (London: Penguin 1991)

— *Bully for Brontosaurus* (London: Penguin, 1992)

— 'The Confusion Over Evolution', *New York Review of Books*, 19 November 1992.

— 'Darwinian Fundamentalism', *New York Review of Books*, 12 June 1997

— *The Mismeasure of Man* (London: Penguin, 1997)

— *Life's Grandeur*, paperback edn. (London: Vintage, 1997; published in USA as *Full House*, 1989)

Gould, Stephen Jay, and Frederick Burkhardt, eds., *Charles Darwin's Letters: A Selection 1825–1859* (Cambridge: Cambridge University Press, 1998)

Gould, Stephen Jay, and Richard Lewontin, 'The Spandrels of San Marco', *Proceedings of the Royal Society B*, vol. 205 (1979), pp. 581–98.

Greenfield, Susan, *The Human Brain* (London: Weidenfeld & Nicolson, 1997)

Haldane, J. B. S., *The Causes of Evolution* (London: Longmans, Green & Co, 1932)

Hamilton, William, 'The Genetical Evolution of Social Behaviour' (I and II), *Journal of Theoretical Biology*, vol. 7 (1964), pp. 1–16 and 17–52

— 'Innate Social Aptitudes of Man: An Approach from Evolutionary Genetics' (ASA Studies 4: *Biosocial Anthropology*, London, 1975; reprinted in *Narrow Roads of Gene Land*)

— *Narrow Roads of Gene Land: The Collected Papers of W. D. Hamilton* (Oxford, W. H. Freeman/Spektrum, 1996)

Hardy, Alister, *Darwin and the Spirit of Man* (London: Collins, 1984)

Harris, Marvin, *Cows, Pigs, Wars and Witches* (New York: Vintage, 1989)

— *Cannibals and Kings* (New York: Vintage, 1991)

Hull, David, *Darwin and His Critics: The Reception of Darwin's*

Theory of Evolution by the Scientific Community (Cambridge, MA: Harvard University Press, 1973)

— *Science as a Process* (London: University of Chicago Press, 1990)

Humphrey, Nicholas, *Soul Searching* (London: Chatto & Windus, 1995)

— 'What shall we Tell the Children?', Amnesty Lecture, Oxford, 21 February 1997.

Huxley, Julian, *Essays in Popular Science* (London: 1926)

James, William, *The Varieties of Religious Experience* (London: Penguin, 1958)

Kitcher, Philip, *Vaulting Ambition* (Cambridge, MA: MIT Press, 1985)

Knauft, Bruce, 'Reconsidering Violence in Simple Human Societies', *Current Anthropology*, vol. 28 (1987), pp. 457–500

Lewontin, Richard, *The Doctrine of DNA* (London: Penguin, 1993)

— 'Billions and Billions of Demons', *New York Review of Books*, 9 January 1997

Machiavelli, Niccolò, *The Prince*, trans. Mark Musa and Peter Bondanella (Oxford: Oxford University Press, 1990)

Mackie, J. L., 'Genes and Egoism', *Philosophy*, vol. 56 (1981), pp. 553–5

Mayr, Ernst, *The Growth of Biological Thought: Diversity, Evolution, and Inheritance* (Cambridge, MA, and London: The Belknap Press of Harvard University Press, 1982)

Midgley, Mary, 'Gene Juggling', *Philosophy*, vol. 54 (Cambridge University Press, 1979), pp. 439–58

— 'Selfish Genes and Social Darwinism', *Philosophy*, vol. 58 (1983), pp. 365–77

— *Evolution as a Religion* (London: Routledge, 1986)

— *Science as Salvation* (London: Routledge, 1994)

— *Beast and Man* (London: Routledge, 1995)

Morgan, Elaine, *The Scars of Evolution* (Oxford: Oxford University Press, 1995)

— *The Descent of the Child* (London: Penguin, 1996)

— *The Descent of Woman* (London: Souvenir Press, 1997)

Morris, Desmond, *The Naked Ape* (London: Vintage, 1994)

Nelkin, Dorothy, 'The Science-Textbook Controversies', *Scientific American*, vol. 234 (April 1976), pp. 33–9

— *The Creation Controversy* (New York and London: W. W. Norton, 1982)

Nelkin, Dorothy, and Susan Lindee, *The DNA Mystique* (New York: W. H. Freeman, 1995)

Pinker, Steven, *How the Mind Works* (London: Allen Lane, 1997)

Ridley, Matt, *The Origins of Virtue* (London: Penguin, 1997)

Rose, Steven, Leon J. Kamin and Richard Lewontin, *Not in Our Genes* (London: Penguin, 1984)

Ruse, Michael, *Darwinism Defended: A Guide to the Evolution Controversies* (Reading, MA: Addison-Wesley, 1982)

— *Taking Darwin Seriously* (Oxford: Blackwell, 1987)

Ruthven, Malise, *The Divine Supermarket* (London: Chatto & Windus, 1989)

Segerstråle, Ullica, 'Colleagues in Conflict', *Biology and Philosophy*, vol. 1 (1986), pp. 53–88

Smith, John Maynard, *The Theory of Evolution* (Cambridge: Cambridge University Press, 1993)

Sperber, Daniel, *Explaining Culture* (Oxford: Blackwell, 1996)

Spufford, Margaret, *Celebration* (London: Mowbray, 1995)

Stapledon, Olaf, *Last and First Men* (Mineola, NY: Dover, 1972)

Tooby, John, Jerome H. Barkow and Leda Cosmides, *The Adapted Mind* (Oxford: Oxford University Press, 1995)

— critique of Gould on: http://www.psych.ucsb.edu/research/cep/

Trivers, Robert, *Social Evolution* (Menlo Park, CA: Benjamin/Cummings, 1985)

Watson, James D., *The Double Helix: A Personal Account of the Discovery of the Structure of DNA* (London: Penguin, 1970)

Williams, George, and Randy Nessé, *Evolution and Healing* (London: Phoenix, 1996)

Wilson, Edward O., *The Insect Societies* (Cambridge, MA: Harvard University Press, 1971)

— *Sociobiology: The New Synthesis* (Cambridge, MA: Harvard University Press, 1975)

— *On Human Nature* (Cambridge, MA: Harvard University Press, 1978)

— *The Diversity of Life* (London: Allen Lane, 1993)

— *Naturalist* (London: Allen Lane, 1995)

— *Consilience* (New York: Alfred A. Knopf, 1998)

Wind, Jan, *The Aquatic Ape: Fact or Fiction?* (London: Souvenir Press, 1991)

INDEX

TOUCHSTONE
SIMON & SCHUSTER

NOAH'S FLOOD
THE NEW SCIENTIFIC DISCOVERIES ABOUT
THE EVENT THAT CHANGED HISTORY

William Ryan & Walter Pitman

'*Noah's Flood* combines folklore with scholarship in a way which is accessible to the ordinary reader. It brings to life a time, like our own, during which sea levels were rising and describes the devastating impact this had on human society. A fascinating read'
TONY ROBINSON

This is the account of a sensational flood, 7,600 years ago that burst through the narrow Bosphorus valley with unimaginable force and poured the Mediterranean's salt water into a vast freshwater oasis. In creating the modern Black Sea this deluge obliterated the homeland of townspeople like us, while expelling survivors into Europe and Mesopotamia and setting the stage for the emergence of the world's first cities and empires.

ISBN   0 684 86137 2
PRICE £8.99